Follow

How to get
2,000 REAL Instagram
followers every month.

R.J. HENDRICKSON

Follow: How to get 2,000 REAL Instagram followers every month.

For permission requests or general inquiries, email the publisher at the following email address: ryanjhendrickson@mail.com.

If you enjoyed this book, please leave an Amazon review and share it with others!

ISBN: 9781718134232 (Paperback)

Cover Design by germancreative

R.J. Hendrickson Publishing

Boston, MA

www.poemwars.com

~

To the community of Poem Wars,

who gave me the courage to take the leap.

~

Do I dare
Disturb the universe?
In a minute there is time
For decisions and revisions which a minute will
reverse.

- T.S. Eliot, *The Love Song of J. Alfred Prufrock*

TABLE OF CONTENTS

<u>Preface</u>

The reason I'm writing this book is because I wish someone had given me a manual to launch my own Instagram when I was starting out.

Those first few days, weeks, months, are painful. You're wandering through the woods in the dark, and there's no flashlight to help you see where you're going. There's no campfire to keep you warm on those cold nights when you're wondering what the hell you're doing. Forging ahead with no direction is terrifying and, luckily, unnecessary.

If I had a road map during those days, weeks, and months, it would have saved me hundreds of hours experimenting, making mistakes that I could have easily avoided if there were just a little more information on what works and what doesn't. There's definitely a path to success in launching a prosperous Instagram page, one that will help you accomplish your dream, be it an active community or a thriving business.

This is your road map. Use this book to confidently navigate that journey. In <u>Part One</u>, I'll tell you the story of how I created my Instagram, the twists and turns I faced and how I overcame them. In <u>Part Two</u>, I'll give you the exact recipe for gaining 2,000 followers every month. And, in <u>Part Three</u>, I'll address relevant Instagram topics brought up over the course of the book in more detail.

And remember - I'm still in the trenches with you. As of the publication of this book, my Instagram community has just reached over 10,000 followers. Since this benchmark, my account has been on the Instagram fast track. Engagement has doubled. Posts are reaching tens and tens of thousands of Instagrammers every day. Followers and likes are flowing in like a rushing river. It's simultaneously gratifying and humbling.

The goal of this book is to simply share with you how I did it: how I grew (and am currently growing) my following by over 2,000 followers every month.

I hope this allows people like myself, anyone who has a passion to share and an audience they want to inspire, to rise to success faster than they ever dreamed possible.

This is my war diary.

- R.J. Hendrickson

Introduction

"The hardest thing is to start."

This idea has been pounded into our heads since grade school.

"Take the leap, then learn to fly."

"A journey of a thousand miles begins with a single step."

Very inspirational stuff. More importantly, it's complete and utter bullshit. The less comfortable truth is:

<u>The hardest thing is to persist.</u>

In the case of gaining Instagram followers (the most likely reason you picked up this book), persistence makes the difference between success and failure, between Insta-famous and instantly irrelevant. But it's not all blood, sweat, and tears. While building a massive Instagram following certainly takes effort, it doesn't take that much effort. It just takes perseverance: habitual and continuous progress. Constant forward movement.

I should know. I built an Instagram following of over 10,000 real, active users in 6 months. In the coming pages, I'll tell you my story. I'll share with you my exact, infallible methods for gaining 2,000 followers or more every month.

This is your Instagram cookbook, a straightforward and easy-to-follow recipe for rapid Insta-fame. If you follow it word by word, it will work. If it doesn't, feel free to contact me and I'll gladly send you a handwritten apology and a full refund. I have an undying faith in my strategies, and I'm excited for you to share in that success too.

The best part?

It will cost you almost nothing. Only the price of this book. I built my entire following for free. Admittedly, I dabbled in paid promotion - Instagram ads, outsourcing my process to automate it. Yet these schemes fell flat. My method always came out on top. Hard work beat immediate gratification every time.

There is one caveat. This book comes with a warning. If you're going to build a large following - gaining influence and the ability to deeply affect your audience on a personal level - you <u>must</u> use that power responsibly. Be a force of good. Spread love, art, connection, beauty, and understanding. Don't succumb to the egotism and vanity that often comes from amassing fans. If you don't think you can handle that responsibility, please close this book. Return it. Throw it away. Delete it.

However, if you believe that you can use these methods with good intentions, creating a page that will positively resonate with your community, adding value to their lives and a little more light to the world, you are in the right place.

So read on, dear reader. Persist.

Progress awaits.

Follow

Part One

POEM

WARS

1.

The Idea

In October of 2017, I had an idea, and I couldn't get it out of my head.

For many years, my secret hobby was to write poetry. For the most part my hobby sat in a tiny red journal on my shelf, or was buried in dusty word documents filed away on my computer's hard drive that hadn't been opened for years. I didn't have the courage to make an attempt at publishing my work. I didn't even have the courage to share my poems with my friends, girlfriends, or family.

After a series of existential crises, I momentarily pushed past my fear and submitted my work to a series of different publications and literary journals. Most didn't respond. Others waited 6 months only to send me polite denial letters.

"Dear Mr. Hendrickson,

Thank you for submitting to The New Yorker. Although we won't be carrying your work in the magazine, we are grateful for the opportunity to read and consider it, and we wish you the best as you keep writing poetry.

Sincerely,

The Editors."

At least they were grateful for the opportunity.

I avoided thinking about the more than $200 in submission fees down the drain, the incalculable cost of coffee from cafés and emotional fuel burnt over months and months of patiently waiting to hear back from publications and editors.

It wasn't approval I was looking for. I already had plenty of that. Friends and family telling me one poem I had written had brought them to tears, or another had transported them back to the playful innocence of first love, the deep loneliness following heartbreak, the wondrous exultation of youth. The feedback, my accolades, the pure volume of creative ideas that popped into my head in a constant stream — they only made the growing feeling of dread worse.

What good was it to be a writer, a poet, an artist, without a way for people to see my work? I imagined myself in a tiny gallery tucked in the back of a tired book store, watching my nonexistent audience walk blissfully past without a second glance.

Without some form of publication, was there any hope for me to be a author? Or, was my passion doomed to be a hobby, something I did in private at a lonely desk in my apartment after leaving the daily prison of a cubicle, accompanied only by a pen and the blank page and a bottle of wine?

Alone.

After that tenth rejection letter, I had enough. I put the dream on the shelf. I again let it gather dust and told myself that

I had to be more "realistic". If I couldn't use my gift the way I wanted to, I had to use it the way *society* wanted me to. My next applications weren't to literary magazines or online publications or poetry contests, but to ad agencies and marketing firms and junior sales positions. I traded inspiration and creative passion for healthcare benefits and a 401k.

And, for more than a year, I let myself be miserable.

Yet a funny thing happened. That inner voice, the one I had convinced myself was a fraud, a hopeless lie—it didn't die. Instead, to my surprise, it grew stronger. What once was a whisper had turned to a shout. It wanted, needed, to be heard.

In a moment of sheer insanity, I decided I would create my own platform - a community to share my poetry with that gave others the opportunity to share their work as well. Why let crusty editors in big NYC offices tell the little guys like me what was good or what wasn't? Unknown writers deserved to be published too. We needed an online sanctuary. Safe behind the glow of our smartphone screens, we could feel a little less afraid. A little less vulnerable.

So I created a name. "The Poet Collective". I bought a web domain, put together a simple Wordpress site with a link to submit poetry, and wrote an impassioned manifesto on the front page. And, over the course of two weeks, I got one submission - a haiku written by my mom. The lesson was clear. It's impossible to create a community if you don't have an audience. I was back to square one.

Mulling over how I could build something people would really engage in, I browsed social media and quickly found my answer:

Instagram.

The platform already had a MASSIVE poetry community that I had largely been unaware of. I had heard of the R.M. Drake's and the Rupi Kaur's, but what I didn't realize was that there were millions and millions of poetry posts tagged with the hope of seeing the light of day in an enormous pool of creative work. Thousands and thousands of poems every day, every hour. Hundreds every second.

I had found my niche, and I had found my platform.

Yet how was I going to get these millions of people to follow me? How could I entice people, convince them, trick them into following a newcomer nobody like myself? How could I get them to join my rebellious little movement?

First things first, the movement needed a name. A better name than "The Poet Collective". One of the many ideas stuck rattling around my head was "Poem Wars". I had no clue as to why I thought it would work. Perhaps it felt like there was some aspect of competition when people shared their work, the winners catching the public eye, the losers getting buried under duck-faced selfies and pictures of Icelandic glaciers.

Only later did the deeper meaning start to become clear, that poetry is an internal war, a fight to capture our tangled emotions and spill them onto a page, to reveal our innermost vulnerabilities to the outside world. Or, perhaps, poetry was a

17

rebellious rejection of a society that requires us to bury our emotions beneath the surface, to push them down beneath empty smiles.

For whatever reason, the name stuck.

Poem Wars was my start, the cliff which I decided to leap from. Yet it was more than a username. The reason I started this journey was to create more than a brand. It was more than validation, more than creating an online image of myself. I was using this platform and trying to build my audience because I was still searching for my identity.

Little did I realize the social media profile would simply be a reflection of who I was. My posts came from my constantly evolving experiences, the captions no more than the thoughts that filled my head as I tried to define my inner being. I was attempting to understand the life I was living, and perhaps find some greater meaning in it.

As I prepared to take that leap, I had no idea what was to come. I couldn't see the bottom, only the horizon. Dreams were about to meet reality.

The one thing I did know was that I was done waiting.

2.

The Leap

Starting was the easy part.

I downloaded the Instagram app, signed up with my email, chose the username Poem_Wars, and added a picture of a fountain pen writing on parchment paper that I had downloaded online. For my bio, I wrote "~ Serving up daily doses of your favorite poetry. ~"

Short. Simple. To the point.

My strategy was equally straightforward: I would collect quotes of my favorite poetry classics, put them over relevant images using a photo editing app, credit the original author, and put the rest of the poem in the caption. The goal was to share beautiful words, but also to educate the "uninformed" Instagram poetry community about the great poems and poets of the past.

It was just as arrogant and boring as it sounds.

The finishing touch? # Hashtags.

I was informed by a close friend that you could add up to thirty # hashtags to every post, and doing so would more or less "reveal" your post to the Instagram community, as hashtags helped direct posts to be organized according to their content.

Essentially, he explained, if you wanted to find poetry on the app you just searched for #poetry and would find a page full of poetry posts, including your own tagged post. The hashtags varied from the simple #poems or #poetryofinstagram, to more complex and niche tags like #typewriterpoetry, #lovepoems, #instapoets, et cetera, et al, ad infinitum.

Having zero followers, I figured this would be one of the best ways to start getting attention - a.k.a. likes and followers. The other method, the more important and effective one, took me much longer to figure out.

My first post was my favorite line from T.S. Eliot's "*The Love Song of J. Alfred Prufrock*".

Do I dare

Disturb the Universe?

In a minute there is time

For decisions and revisions

Which a minute will reverse.

I appreciated the irony. This was my leap. I was attempting to disturb my own personal universe, to not reverse my decision to start a page in my limitless insecurity and self-doubt.

It got about 10 likes. I was ecstatic. Then: I got 1 follower.

I almost shit my pants in pure happiness.

As clichéd as it sounded, I knew every single follower counted. That one follower told me that I could get 2 followers, and then 4 and then 8 and then 100. Those 10 likes meant I could get 20 and then 40 and then 1,000. Finally - an audience.

Yet to get likes and followers, I needed posts. This would be where persistence came in. I made another post the next day - Sylvia Plath's "*Daddy*":

Bit my pretty red heart in two.

I was ten when they buried you.

At twenty I tried to die

And get back, back, back to you.

I thought even the bones would do.

Dark stuff. Gritty. More or less word-porn for serious poets.

It got about 5 likes.

My heart sunk. *It's not working. I'm giving up.*

I was suddenly struck by the seemingly obvious revelation: maybe I wasn't getting any likes because I didn't have any followers, and I didn't have any followers because I didn't follow anyone. I immediately followed 30 of the biggest poets in my niche.

Then I went to sleep.

I woke up the next day with 5 followers. *Huzzah!* After, every subsequent post I made, I followed another 30 people in my niche. I would find the profile of some Insta-famous poet and follow the suggested accounts at the top of their page.

The more I followed, the more would follow me. Or their followers followed me. The more followers I had, the more likes I had. Maybe it was an Instagram algorithm. Or maybe my followers were liking my posts. Maybe my content was just getting better. Maybe it was magic, or divine intervention.

I was just happy progress was being made. Next, Bukowski's *"Roll the Dice"*:

If you're going to try

go all the way.

there is no other feeling

like that.

you will be alone with the gods

and the nights will flame

with fire.

People loved it. Inspiration worked. Check.

Next, e.e. cummings -

here is the deepest secret

nobody knows

i carry your heart (i carry it in my heart)

Like, like, follow, follow - romance worked. Check.

Robert Frost, Langston Hughes, Dylan Thomas - the more I posted, the more accounts I followed, the more likes I would get and the more people followed me. The hardest part was finding the poetry and designing the posts. It was annoying. My laziness was tired of doing work.

Poem Wars was on its way to success. The ball was rolling. If I kept going the same direction, at the same pace, it would grow - about 300 followers a month, but it would grow. And that wasn't enough for me. I wanted to create a huge community, something massive, with *impact*.

And, caught up in my own ideas and ambitions, I forgot about gravity. I forgot that what goes up can also come down.

3.

<u>The Pivot</u>

As well as Poem Wars was doing, it wasn't exploding. I stopped posting as much because of the stress of the holidays, and the 400 followers that I had built up since the beginning of November 2017 had gone down to less than 350 by Christmastime.

It was time to pivot, to come up with a new and better strategy, or else my account was going to hit the ground and be broken to pieces. Without progress, I'd lose the will to keep persisting. With all of my momentum gone, I went back to drawing board.

To start, I took a step back and looked objectively at what <u>was</u> working and what <u>wasn't</u> working.

Both didn't take long to identify.

For one, my hashtags were too vague. #Poems had millions of posts. How could my 20 likes possibly stand out? Secondly, all those hashtags under my posts looked like absolute crap. Not only did it look desperate, it looked like I had no idea what I was doing (which, at the time, I didn't).

Secondly, for every 10 people I followed, only 1 would follow back. A few would follow organically after seeing and liking my posts. However, my "return on investment" was laughable. 10% was not good enough. And it was messing up my follower to following ratio. My account was getting pudgy. I was looking like a try-hard.

I turned to others for help - to people who were far more social media savvy than me, ones who had already gone through these trials and tribulations and came out the other side more informed.

Their advice was simple and unanimous:

a) refine your hashtags

b) update your "follow" method

c) groom your follower vs. following ratio

It was perfect advice, but would require a complete overhaul of my system. I took a deep breath and jumped back in. The first week of January became my testing grounds, a time to pivot and recreate my page. This one week would ultimately redefine my method, leading me to a whole new level of success beyond anything I had dreamed possible.

My first step: **refine my hashtags**.

Instead of vague, general hashtags like #poems, I found 30 *relevant* and *highly active* tags that were not only specific but also had a high volume of posts. Why? Because it would be much easier to stick out in a collective pool of 500-1000 total posts per day, or one every 1 or 2 minutes, than to try to get a second glance when there was a post every other second.

My focus was on hashtags in my niche, the poetry community, that had more than 50,000 posts total (meaning, total posts since the first use of that hashtag) but less than 1 million total posts. After a little research, I had my perfect 30 tags. The result? Nearly **double** the likes per post. 20 likes became 38 likes. People apparently had easier access to see my posts, and it helped dramatically.

As for the eyesore of seeing 30 hashtags in the caption under each post, a friend gave me fantastic advice: just put 5 vertical "dots" above the hashtags, one per line, with the hashtags underneath. Then, rather then put the hashtag list into my caption, I should just paste it in the comment section of my post immediately after posting.

Here's an example:

.

.

.

.

.

#poemwars #poetry #poetrycommunity #typewriterpoetry #bikinis #friedchicken #amsterdam #hairspray #gymnastics #insurancefraud #gardengnomes #sextips #soap #etc

When they're in the comment section, he explained, it would still apply the hashtags to my post, but keep them hidden in the comments. It was a phenomenal hack, and easy as pie. (This process will be covered in detail in Part Two)

But why the dots? It seemed that because the dots added to the length of the comment, it forced the comment to be hidden. Rather than show up under the post, I would just see ellipses (…), unless I clicked on the comment section, in which case it would reveal itself. I could also have used other symbols, such as asterisks (*) or tildes (~), which also had the same effect, but I thought the dots looked the cleanest.

Doing this didn't necessarily increase my total followers or likes, but it definitely upped the aesthetic of my page and posts significantly. Yes - people could still see my hashtags, but because they were hidden in the comments, they looked less glaringly obvious and desperate. It was just prettier. I was starting to feel like more of a professional Instagrammer, and as my confidence built, my following grew.

The next step: **update my "follow" method.**

Another good friend of mine, who has multiple social media ventures with hundreds of thousands of followers, gave me a very simple recommendation. Rather than liking posts that already have thousands of likes, and following accounts that already have tens of thousands of followers, he said to focus on the little guys. All I had to do was like recent posts that barely had any likes yet, and to follow accounts that had very few followers, ones that were still trying to grow. In essence, accounts just like mine.

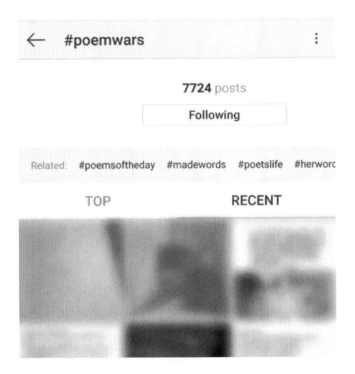

The reason became obvious. Young accounts with few followers were FAR more likely to follow me back. Why? Because I was now one of their only fans. And that's a big deal. I thought about it. When I was starting out, the first likes that came to my posts were like miracles, each new a follower a saint. I followed those very people back and liked all of their recent posts. I became one of their groupies.

Reversing that idea, people in the same position would feel the same about me. By being their first, second, third, even tenth like, they would be much more likely to follow me back and like my posts. For one, they'd feel indebted to me. I was one of the original supporters for their post. Secondly, and more importantly, they just posted, so they were likely still very active on the app - far more so than someone who posted an hour ago. In this way, I was greatly increasing my visibility.

It paid to be shameless about the process, at least to start. Liking and following a massive amount of people in one fell swoop was easy. After every post I made, I'd click on one of the hashtags I had copied and pasted. Then I'd scroll down the recent posts within that hashtag, double-tap the post to like it, and then press the little blue "follow" button to the right of their username to follow them (without having to take the time to actually go to their profile).

I have large hands and fingers, so hitting the little "follow" button without accidentally clicking on something else took a considerable amount of time and practice, but persistence made perfect.

The results were immediate: another **double** the amount of likes on every post I made, and **double** the amount of daily followers.

The final step: **groom my "ratio".**

I repeatedly rejected this advice starting out. Who cared if I was following more people than were following me? I was only looking at how many followers I had and how much people engaged with each post. I kept seeing my engagement go up, so I didn't bother to slim down the amount of accounts I followed.

As I followed more and more people after every post, I started to see my ratio tip. I looked desperate. Yes, 900 people followed me, but I was following almost 2,000. I knew that this number would only grow and grow as I moved forward, and I needed to figure out how to keep things on an even plane.

I started by going into the "Following" section of my page and began to indiscriminately unfollow people. After a day of unfollowing 250 people, I took a break. The next day, I had lost 50 followers. I quickly realized - people were aware that I just dropped out of their following, and were not happy. So they booted me. Furthermore, they probably would no longer like my posts or engage with my page anymore.

This method would only lead my account to self-destruct. Was it worth losing followers just to slim down and maintain my "image"? Would it be worth limiting my impact just because of the egotism and vanity of wanting to look popular? To look like people cared about me more than I cared about them?

No. The numbers were clear: people were engaging whether I followed a ton of people or not. I would later find out that a major portion of your fans rarely visit your profile page. They rarely look at how many people you follow. They simply follow you and see your posts show up on their home page. And if they enjoy the posts, they engage like crazy.

However, there had to be a middle ground. There had to be a way to maintain my engagement, keep my followers, yet not let the amount of accounts I followed become too bloated. But how?

After searching the app store, I found a few apps that gave me information on my account's following. They informed me of the people that I followed who didn't follow me back, and allowed me to unfollow these people straight from the app. I could even batch unfollow them, dozens at a time.

Because I was unfollowing people who didn't follow me in the first place, I didn't see a drop in my numbers. My amount of followers stayed the same. These accounts weren't engaged with mine in the first place, and cutting them out changed nothing. This came as a huge relief, and doing so quickly slimmed down my account, leaving me with more followers than accounts that I was following. I maintained every few days, cutting out the duds using the unfollowing apps with minimal effort.

And, as I continued to post and apply my method, my engagement only grew and grew - faster than ever before.

It had taken me nearly 2 months to get to 400 followers, and suddenly in only 1 week I already had more than 1000 total followers. Before, I was getting 1 like back per 5 posts that I liked, and 1 follower per 10 accounts that I followed. Now, the game had changed. Liking AND following simultaneously increased those stats dramatically. After implementing my new strategy, I got 1 like for every 2 that I liked/followed, as well as 1 new follower for every 4 that I liked/followed.

On top of that, organic followers were flowing in like crazy. Accounts I had never seen or interacted with were following and liking and commenting. My efforts had cast a wide net, and the surge of interest in my posts due to my new method seemed to have caused Instagram to spread them farther than before. They were now being viewed by a much larger audience

I had more than doubled my user engagement and follower rate overnight.

Yet, there was still one missing piece.

My page was growing again, faster than ever before. But something still wasn't quite right. My entire process felt scattered, lacking a central purpose. My "movement" didn't feel like it was was moving in a direction. My "rebellion" didn't seem rebellious.

The page still had no identity.

4.

The Community

Poem Wars started as a way to share work and build a collective of engaged poets. Yet here I was posting crusty poetry from dead poets who hadn't been around for decades, words that were hundreds of years old. How had I gone astray? Where did I misstep?

In another full-blown existential crisis, I went for a walk to clear my head. I walked down the city sidewalks as evening struck and a hush went over the streets. People left their workplaces and filed into their houses, cooking dinner and watching the newest show on Netflix. They gathered in crowded bars that lined the moonlit boulevards, strangers sharing the ambiance of evening music and foaming beers.

And, as I walked past these local haunts and the cozy fires warming gentle houses, it suddenly became clear that I was entirely missing the point.

What I had been sharing wasn't as relevant as what was standing right in front of me the whole time: the work of the community.

I wasn't bringing people together. I wasn't connecting them, showing them the beauty of the written words all around them. The beauty that I saw every time I opened the app. Current poetry.

I nervously screenshotted a post that I loved and cropped it, wrote out the appropriate tags to give credit to the author, and posted it.

the monsters under the bed
are hiding too.

I left Instagram momentarily to text my friend, and then reopened the app. It had been 5 minutes. I hadn't liked or followed anyone yet.

I already had 4 followers and 20 likes.

Holy shit.

A sudden fear hit me, washing away the excitement. *Would the poet be okay with me re-posting his work?* A half hour later he commented, "Thank you so much for the feature." The fear washed away and excitement returned.

Likes and followers flowed in like a river. I had never seen so much interaction, and spent the rest of the night stunned, finishing a bottle of wine and racking my mind as to why the change had such a drastic effect.

The next day I re-posted again. The poet thanked me and even put me in his Insta-story. Even more likes and follows. The next day, another re-post. More likes. More followers. More gratitude. In combination with my strategy of liking and following recent posts, I again more than doubled my 1,000 person following in less than two weeks.

What I had begun to post was <u>relevant</u> to the community. These poets were currently breathing, not hidden in the pages of old books. They were creating endless content every day, content I didn't have to search for. Many of these poets already had a lot of likes and followers. Their work had passed the test of Instagram and was received with open arms. Others had few, but just by posting their work I gave them a chance to become more visible to potential readers. Everything about it felt right.

It's essential to know what people like, to travel through the veins of the collective consciousness. Does that mean you need to conform to what's popular to get a following? Certainly not. People love new and rebellious content, posts that they've never seen before.

However, when I started posting the work of real, live Instagram poets, I was truly connecting with the community. I was sharing in the love of new, relevant art, the very reason people came to the app to share their work in the first place. I had been avoiding connection out of a fear of rejection, yet connecting with the community was the most nourishing thing I could do.

And it paid dividends.

A few posts later, I hit my first jackpot. It will happen a few times in the beginning if you stick with it, then more and more frequently, but your first one is like discovering buried treasure. It's pure magic.

The poem wasn't that different than others I posted. Maybe it was timing, or it just hit the right chord. It is hard to know why something works. That's the exciting part, the gamble, the true mystery.

> *There was a silence*
>
> *in her eyes*
>
> *not fear,*
>
> *but a sadness*
>
> *she had grown*
>
> *comfortable with.*

Three hours later the post had 700+ likes. I'm not sure if the poet ever saw it, if she ever knew that my sharing of her work had broken down any sense of limitation that I still carried in my mind. That jackpot gave me a new dose of life, a sudden surge of energy.

I was no longer hiding.

5.

<u>The Result</u>

Poem Wars went from 350 followers around Christmas of 2017 to 1,000 on January 13th, 2018. On February 13th, Poem Wars had over 3,000 followers.

As of the date of publishing this book, I've hit well over 10,000 followers.

I didn't post for 4 days straight and still gained 40 followers a day. The page has been getting about 60-70 followers per post, and a minimum of 600 likes per post (with an average range of about 800-1,200). There are usually 15-20 comments per post, and sometimes substantially more. My engagement is beyond my wildest dreams, with reach and impressions numbering in many tens of thousands. I've hit over 22 jackpots.

Six months in, I'm thinking of the future. Will I hit 25,000 followers by the end of the year? How do I respond to all of the comments and direct message's (DM's) - over 15 a day? The tag #poemwars has now been used on over 8,000 posts. My page has been directly tagged (@poemwars) almost 10,000 times.

Six months in, and I don't know what the hell happened. In many ways, I think I wrote this book for myself - to figure out why and how it all came together the way it did, and to try to let people in on the secret.

I'm about to publish a compilation of the Poem Wars community's poetry called "Bloom." It will feature the work of 70 poets, poems of loss, heartbreak, and how we learn to begin again after traversing those painful experiences. Thousands of poets submitted incredible work, many contacting me with humbling praise and gratitude. The tag created specifically for submissions, #iaminbloom, was tagged over 700 times in less than a month.

Yet it's not just a numbers game. Instagram is a community of living, breathing people. They are looking to share a bit of themselves with the world, be it their thoughts or their muscles or their tan bodies in skimpy bikinis or stunning pictures of their travels or their beautiful, soulful, vulnerable words.

I'm growing to love it.

This page is not just an obsession. It has also become a release, a form of therapy. The conversations I've had with my community have been both heartbreaking and uplifting.

People have shared stories of attempted suicide, experiences of abuse, moments of deep pain and loneliness. They've also told me of how they overcame those moments, how they have undergone profound shifts, a renewal and rebirth that has cleansed their spirit and liberated their souls from years of suffering.

Poetry - expressing themselves on the page and sharing it with the world - has helped them heal. Having an audience has allowed them to leave isolation and reconnect.

From love to loss, we all have stories to tell and people to tell them to. Our following - our audience - is more than a number. They are more than likes and comments, more than metrics of engagement and reach.

They're our family.

Follow

Part Two

The

Recipe

<u>"The Instagram Method"</u>

<u>A Practical Guide</u>

For those like myself that need to see a practical, actionable, step-by-step process, I will use this chapter to outline my entire method from start to finish. Even if you didn't read Part One of this book, you'll have all the tools here that you need to launch your Instagram successfully and grow it rapidly. Still, you should go back and read it. It will only help your understanding.

This method is universal. Whether you are an artist, entrepreneur, brand, influencer, photographer, actor, model, musician, puppeteer, or internet troll - follow this process step-by-step and it will work.

Of course, it may be necessary to fine-tune my advice to appropriately apply to your niche. Take creative license where you see fit, yet the core ideas will remain the same. Use them strategically.

Without further ado, here's the recipe.

1. <u>Step One:</u>

<u>Create an Instagram Account.</u>

Yep. It's not rocket science. Use your email and create a password to login with. Easy enough, right?

Although it seems stupid to even include this as part of the method, many avoid doing this simple step to delay action. Just do it, if you haven't already. And do it now. It will get you motivated.

Don't listen to those nagging doubts.

"Maybe nobody will want to follow me! Maybe nobody will like my posts! Maybe my page will completely flounder and my dream will be destroyed and I will have to move to another country out of shame!"

Breathe. Say your fears out loud. Write them out. Just get them out of your head and you'll see how ridiculous they are.

And, now that you've done that, sign up for a damn account.

2. **Step Two:**

Pick a Niche.

I would hope you've already thought at least a little about this. Your niche - the specific Instagram community you wish to be a part of - will be the lifeblood of your page and the source of your following.

Don't let this idea be vague. Be as focused as possible. Is your niche about pets? If yes - what type of pets? If dogs - what type of dogs? Puppies?

There you go. You're creating an Instagram page focusing on puppies. Not pets, or dogs, but *specifically* puppies. This will help you with many of the later steps - creating the perfect username, bio, hashtag selection, style - and will set your feet firmly on the ground to start moving forward. If you fail to pick a concentrated niche, one that you love and ideally know something about, then you will fail to get a following. Period.

My niche is poetry. More specifically, *poetry curation*: collecting and sharing the poetry of others. I picked it because poetry is something I love and am passionate about, and I wanted more of an opportunity to read and share poetry.

It can be very difficult to decide which hobby or interest best suits an Instagram page. Maybe you have a lot of hobbies and interests, or maybe you have a specific few but love them all too equally to choose. Or maybe you have no hobbies or interests, in which case there are probably more important things for you to work on than creating a successful Instagram page.

Luckily, picking a niche is simpler than you might think. It requires that you make 3 straightforward decisions. It will take less than 5 minutes, and will leave you with a warm fuzzy feeling when you're done. Decide rapidly. The faster the better. This will override your worried, conscious mind and let your far-more-capable instincts pick the best candidate.

Now get out a piece of paper.

A. What hobbies are you most passionate about? Do your best to list no more than the top 5 things.

B. Of these passions, which comes to you the most naturally? Meaning, which requires the least amount of effort for you to do, and do well?

C. Are other people passionate about it too? Is there an audience or community who share your passion and would connect with it?

I'll elaborate by using myself as an example.

A. What hobbies am I most passionate about?

i. Photography

ii. Films (making and watching them)

iii. Creating and consuming delicious food/drinks

iv. Music

v. Writing poetry

All of these things make me extremely happy. If I could choose only 5 activities in my life to experience and share with others, it would be those.

B. *Which, of these passions, comes most easily to you?*

i. **Photography.** I love it, but I'm too nit-picky about getting the perfect lighting, angles, colors… it would take too long and I'd be facing a lot of competition. After all, Instagram is largely a photo-sharing app.

ii. **Filmmaking.** Nit-picky doesn't even touch the surface. A video post a day would be a miracle. In terms of effort, this would be the most colossal.

iii. **Food.** I'd rather eat or drink it than post it.

iv. **Music.** I'm still fostering my inner Bob Dylan. And he's not for the public.

v. **Poetry.** It's quick. I love it. I could write a bad haiku every minute.

Read this recipe

You will find Instagram fame

Love will fill your heart

It's not hard. It's fun. It makes me excited. But, the question is…

C. *Does poetry have an Instagram audience?*

Yes. Millions and millions of posts. Thousands and thousands of Instagram poets. Hundreds and hundreds of hashtags.

"But but but," you say, *"how could I possibly stand out amongst the millions of rival accounts? How would I ever be noticed, relevant, loved?"*

Read on, my fine-feathered friends, and all of your questions will be answered.

3. **Step Three:**

Pick a Username.

This is another make-or-break element. It will make a huge difference in your following. Give yourself a leg up and do it correctly from the get-go. You can always change your username as you go (as long as it hasn't already been taken), but you risk losing some of your audience in the process as they'll no longer recognize your account when you post.

A good username requires 4 essential qualities.

A. It's relevant. Your username should, in long or short, relate to your niche, giving your potential audience a sense of what they are about to view when they click on your account.

B. It's memorable. A username like *"fashionable_4372"* is lame. Boring and forgettable (sorry if you're reading this and this is your username, but the truth makes you stronger). There are hundreds of other fashion and style accounts out there with the same idea. However, let's consider the username *"the_femme_fashionista"* - it's memorable and it's relevant. It gives the audience a clear sense of what you might be posting on your page: female fashion and style. This is mainly accomplished because:

C. It's simple. The username doesn't have a massive jumble of letters and numbers. It uses an underscore ("_") or period (".") to separate words or letters, enhancing readability. Simple means memorable, and memorable means relevant. However - most importantly:

D. It's cool. Maybe you disagree. But "*the_femme_fashionista*" is certainly cooler than "*fashionable_4372*". Don't settle. Be bold. Be mysterious. Be sexy. Make a statement. I could have used a username like "*poem_posts_22*" or "*the.page.of.poetry*", but these aren't as interesting or cool.

Separate yourself from the masses.

This is your first opportunity. More will come as you read on, but this is one of the best foundations. If your username can get people to view your page, it's done its job successfully. I don't think anybody knows what the hell *Poem_Wars* means. They just know when they click on it they'll see something having to do with poetry and perhaps something gritty (Robot battles? Medieval warfare?). They ponder - how do these two things relate?

Probably should click and find out.

To create a username, simply:

1. Go to your page by clicking your profile picture in the bottom right corner of your homepage.

2. Click "Edit Profile" at the top

3. Write out your Username. (If it is already taken, Instagram will prompt you to choose another one)

NOTE: This is where you will also write out your chosen name, your bio, attach a website or link, and add contact options.

✕ **Edit Profile** ✓

Change Photo

Name

Poem Wars

Username

poem_wars

Website

Website

Bio

~ Serving up daily doses of your favorite poetry. ~
🖋
Thanks to everyone who submitted to "Bloom"! 🦋

Page   Poem Wars

Category   Publisher

Contact Options

Private Information

E-mail Address

submissions@poemwars.com

4. **Step Four:**

Title Your Page.

Easy enough. Your username minus the symbols. *"poem_wars"* becomes "Poem Wars". *"the_femme_fashionista"* becomes "The Femme Fashionista". Don't over think it. Because your title doesn't need to be unique (like your username does), you have the liberty to elaborate more. For instance, *"j.k_photography"* becomes "John Kelley Photography".

Your title should give context to your username, all the while solidifying your identity. What should people refer to your page as? "The *J dot k underscore photography* page is super badass!" Or, "John Kelley's photography page is super badass!" Again, keep it simple, memorable, relevant, and cool. Not much else to it.

Your page title can be created in the "Name" section when you click on "Edit Profile", directly above the "Username" section.

Moving on.

5. **<u>Step Five:</u>**

<u>Write a Bio.</u>

Ah. The dreaded bio. How could you possibly describe yourself, in all of your glory, in only 150 characters? How could you do your page justice, to express the wonder and beauty and inspiration of your earth-shattering content?

My recommendation is to keep it short and direct. At least to start. Do it in a simple sentence. "~ Serving up daily doses of your favorite poetry ~" with a fountain pen emoji. It gets the point across, and allows you to stop worrying about it. There are far more important steps to worry about.

"But but but that's not utilizing all of the characters!" you say. So what? You can always change your bio later. And guess what? <u>People don't really care about bios.</u> Sometimes, frankly, they're annoying to read. People care about your posts - your content. Stop worrying about your bio and instead focus that mental effort on your posts.

Most importantly, you don't really know what your page is yet. After 10, even 20 posts, you'll start to have a better idea of its true identity. Once you reach that point, then you can reconsider your bio. For now, we just want to hit the ground running as quickly as possible.

Your bio can be created in the "Bio" section when you click on "Edit Profile", directly below the "Website" section.

6. <u>Step Six:</u>

<u>Choose a Profile Picture.</u>

Your profile picture is the final cornerstone of your brand. While people will primarily define you by your work, and reference you by your username, a profile picture holds great power in attracting an audience to your account.

I experimented early on with finding the right image for Poem Wars. I started with a picture of a fountain pen. Very lame. I soon switched to something more abstract, a logo of sorts that had a patterned geometric design to it. However it was too vague to really make out, and didn't make much of an impression.

It suddenly hit me that although Poem Wars was a general curation account, people are pulled in by a personal connection. For this reason, seeing a face in the profile picture would create a real, human element for an audience to relate to. Of course, I wasn't going to put my own face. So I searched for a silhouette of a woman, something intriguing yet tasteful.

It worked. I brought in almost twice the amount of followers over the next week (this is when my numbers were still very low, however). Strangely enough - most of them were women. You would think all of the creepy male Instagrammers would be sucked in by a picture of a female on the account. And they often are.

Yet it seemed that women felt more comfortable with the account because of that image. There was something less imposing about it, something welcoming and not overly branded. Even after designing an official Poem Wars logo, I didn't change it from that silhouetted woman. It worked, and I've learned not to fix what isn't broken.

The key to choosing a good profile picture is to think about how you want to visually represent your account, both encapsulating it's content but also creating more meaning surrounding the account's central purpose. If you're a landscape photographer, perhaps put one of your best photos, one that best showcases your signature style. For models and influencers, find the perfect pose or most polished headshot. For writers or poets, there's a few options, however people seem to respond best to a simple photo portrait of your face - something intimate and direct, perhaps staring straight into the camera or off in the distance. Mysterious yet soulful.

Experiment. See what works best. Over time, like all facets of building an Instagram, the best idea will stick. Change it up until you find one that feels right.

Your profile picture can be created when you click on "Edit Profile", directly above the "Name" section.

Just click "Change Photo" at the top and import something from your gallery.

7. <u>**Step Seven:**</u>

<u>**Pick Your Hashtags.**</u>

Hashtags? What are those? How could they possibly be useful in gaining 2,000 followers a month?

Welcome to 2018. Hashtags (#'s) are the difference between getting your page off the ground versus puttering as your engine fails. If your page is an airplane in this metaphor, hashtags are the fuel. At least to start - over time they become less necessary to keep you airborne. But don't neglect them. They are a powerful tool in gaining <u>visibility</u>, one of the key factors that will bring you to 2,000 followers a month. So don't roam about the main cabin until the captain turns off the seat belt sign, and listen closely.

Instagram lets you post 30 hashtags per post. Your first task is to find your 30. This is going to take a little bit of time, but not *that* much time, and it will be time well spent. You'll more or less never have to compile hashtags again. Just copy and paste them.

As described in Part One, hashtags are used to categorize your content and organize them into # pages, on which you can see everything posted which added that particular hashtag to the post description or as a comment under the post. If, for instance, you post something containing *#poetry* in the description, like "check out my newest *#poetry*!!!", then your post will show up on the #poetry page - along with more than a million other posts (over 20 million, to be exact).

Given that visibility is key, # pages with millions upon millions of posts won't get you very far. Your posts will immediately be buried under the sheer volume of content being churned out on Instagram every 10 seconds. Your target is #'s that have between 50,000 to 1 million posts. To find the amount of posts per hashtag, simply search for the hashtag (like *#poetry*) and you will see that number at the top of the category.

So - how do you know which ones to pick? It's simple. Find posts that you like, ones that are similar to the type of content you'd like to post on your own account. Many of those posts (but not all) will include a series of hashtags attached. Pull out a notepad, and click on one at a time. If the hashtag has between 50,000 - 1 million posts in it, put it on your list.

Keep going until you have 30 or so, looking at a variety of relevant posts to build your lists. Make sure that the #'s you pick actually contain posts similar to yours on the page. If they do, yours will find relevance within that sub-community, which will naturally increase your likes and followers.

Here's a list of the ones I currently use on all my posts:

#iaminbloom #poemwars #spilledink #bymepoetry #omypoetry #poems #poetry #poetsofig #wordswithkings #wordswithqueens #poemsofinstagram #typewriterpoetry #poetryisnotdead #poetrysociety #poetryporn #poeticsoul #poetscorner #poemaday #spilledthoughts #writeon #herheartpoetry #quotesaboutlife #quotesgram #poet #poetrytribe #createeveryday #poemsofig #poetsofinstagram #poetrycommunity #poetryislife

It might sound tedious, but collecting the perfect 30 hashtags will save you a lot of effort in the long-run, and vastly boost your visibility from the get-go. I put all of my hashtags into a notepad on my mobile devices, like "notes" on Apple products, "memo" on Android, or Evernote (my go-to, as it is uploaded to the cloud and syncs across all devices). Then I just copy and paste.

Once you've collected all of these, you're ready for the next step.

8. **Step Eight:**

Choose the Style of Your Posts.

Okay. Yes. I know. This is a hard one. But you've come this far, haven't you? It's easier than you think to pick your style, especially when you break it down into easy steps. Our key mantra in this process:

"Good artists copy. Great artists steal."

At first you're going to make relatively unoriginal posts. They'll be a little derivative, imitations, not very separate from the crowd. That's okay. You'll discover your personal style over time as you continue the process. Yet for now, you have to start somewhere, and the best place to start is with identifying and copying posts that appeal to your personal taste.

Remember those posts that you used to figure out your hashtags? You get to milk them for more than just a few tags. You picked them because, stylistically, you felt they were most similar to what you want to post. So, naturally, you should reverse-engineer them and style your posts to be similar.

Similar, but not *the same*. Just different enough to make them your own. It's relieving to know you don't have to come up with everything on your own. There are millions of posts to help guide you, to serve as rubrics for how to successfully launch your own page. All the resources you need are already in your hands. Pick your top 3 favorite posts or post styles.

If you're trying to post photos, you can use the same lighting, framing, or filters, but try to use content that is <u>you</u>. Pick content you personally connect with - be it pictures of food, workout selfies, or picturesque landscape photography. Copy the style of the posts you love, but add a little flavor of personality to them that makes each post unique. Eventually, as your style evolves, you'll have a better idea what these flavors are and you can enhance and refine them. Remember:

"Good artists copy. Great artists steal."

Be bold. Be shameless. However, in the case of writing, poetry, or re-posting, NEVER plagiarize. This is a cardinal sin. It isn't just disrespectful; it could get you banned. Give credit where credit is due - in the caption (which we'll cover shortly) - tag the original Instagrammer with an @[their username] and some love.

As you know, my content comes from re-posting the work of others. It is not my original work. I am a curator. My particular skill is that I pick standout poetry that other people connect with - but I <u>always</u> give credit to the author. It's not copying. It's stealing. Stealing in a nice way, where I simultaneously promote their pages and my own.

People don't mind that type of mutualism as long as they are appropriately credited. Often, the poets I re-post get significantly more visibility by being featured on my page. Not a single user has reached out to me in anger about re-posting their work. Some that already have huge followings (100k+) will actually reach out and express gratitude.

However you decide to style your post, remember: this is an evolving process. Your page's identity will solidify as you examine your personal tastes and your audience's tastes. With every post, you'll get closer and closer to the mark. Don't be consumed about perfecting your image from the start. It will emerge over time. Chip away day after day, and the marble will suddenly form a refined statue.

9. <u>Step Nine:</u>

<u>Design Your First Post.</u>

Here we go. Breathe. You've got this.

My basic commandment with posting is that while it's generally better to post something rather than post nothing, it's better to post nothing than to post a piece of crap.

We are aiming for <u>quality</u> on our posts, not <u>perfection</u>. Perfectionism will destroy you when it comes to Instagram. Why? If you need a post to be perfect, you'll post about ten times a year. Believe me. I've actually done that. It is (in retrospect) shamefully pathetic, and moreover it's a mentality than can cripple more than just the health of your social media - it can put most of the good things in your life on halt.

So, back to posting. You've **1)** created an account, **2)** picked your niche, and **3)** have a relevant, memorable, impactful username. You also **4)** decided on the title of your page and **5)** wrote a simple but effective bio. Then, you **6)** uploaded a quality profile picture, **7)** chose your 30 perfect hashtags, and **8)** identified the specific style of your posts.

Wonderful. Brilliant. Praise [insert religious deity]. Now - how do we actually design a post? Simple: take a beautiful picture. A cute selfie. Write a thought provoking poem. Film a perfect workout. Prep a delicious plate of foix gras. Nail a cliff-side Sayanasana Scorpion yoga pose.

Okay - obviously, it's not that easy. Especially the cliff-side Scorpion pose. Unfortunately, this is one of the harder parts, but it's not as hard as the persistence thing. As I said before, starting doesn't have to be that hard. By extension, your first post should be the easiest thing for you to post.

What is that one thing that made you think you could start a successful Instagram in the first place? That picture or video or poem or quote or painting or rap or dance or pristinely crafted chocolate truffle cake that made you ponder, *maybe **I** could do that!*

Well, post *that*.

Don't even think about it. Keep it simple. Just take that image, that video, that piece of writing and put it on the chopping block to post. Even something you've already created. Use Instagram's built in filters, cropping, text functions - whatever basic tools you need that are already on the app. Or, download a 3rd party photo design app that can help you do something a little more refined (more on this in Part 3).

Only give yourself a countdown of **10 minutes** to prep the post for Instagram. No more. We're training ourselves in the key advice of this step. Post quality, but at least post *something*. 10 minutes is more than enough time to fashion a post of quality worth sharing with the world. We're talking about Instagram. Do you think the majority of users who use the app know the difference between something good and something incredible?

Answer: No, they don't.

The masses look at likes, follows, and memorable, standout posts that have <u>frequency</u> and <u>consistency</u>. These elements will give you the most visibility. And, for the millionth time, visibility is key.

So - you've designed your post in 10 minutes or less, and you feel that magical feeling. You are nearly ready to post your first Instagram post.

To make a post:

1. Click the "+" button at the bottom center of your Instagram app.

2. Insert a photo or video from your gallery, take a photo, or create a video.

3. Press "Next" in the top right corner.

4. Apply your filters by clicking through the options provided. You can manage the available filters by scrolling through them all the way to the right and clicking the "Manage" button.

5. Additionally, you can edit by pressing "Edit" at the bottom. This will allow you to use a variety of basic editing tools, such as cropping, contrast adjustment, saturation, and more.

6. When you're done editing your photo, press "Next" in the top right corner, which will bring you to the final page before the post is ready to share. Here you can write your caption, tag people or locations, and share to other social media - all of which will be covered in the next few steps.

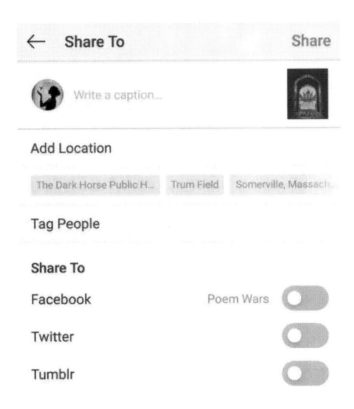

10. __Step Ten:__

__Write the Caption.__

Once again, don't over think this. People often don't read a post's caption. They mainly care about the post, the image, the words contained in the image (if any). Not the caption.

That being said, the caption is the cherry on top. It is your last little *coups de grâce*, a final moment to share you personality, spread your message, or convey your brand.

My captions for Poem Wars are exceedingly basic. I take the words I've posted and just write them out underneath with quotations. At times, I'll also utilize that space to promote a book or call for submissions to a poetry contest.

The styles of captions vary depending on your niche, so examine the captions of posts you love that are similar to yours. This will help you brainstorm options.

For instance, if the poem is the one above, I'll write:

~ *"Don't be afraid to be afraid. We fear the night until we see the moon."* ~

Then I credit the author beneath: "by *@r.j.hendrickson*". The "*@*" creates a tag, which turns the username "*r.j.hendrickson*" into a clickable link. Then, if you click the tag, it will bring you directly to the *r.j.hendrickson* page.

← **Share To** Share

 ~ "Don't be afraid to be afraid. We fear the night until we see the moon." ~
by @r.j.hendrickson

Add Location

Write something short, meaningful, and relevant that adds value to the post rather than detracts or distracts. Give context to an image, perhaps write about the location or circumstance, a micro-story of what we are seeing. Maybe it will be the recipe for the dish you posted, lyrics to a song, info about a product or brand, the name of the photographer who took the photo or the model featured in the post.

Don't worry if it's perfect. Just write the thing (and don't forget to spell check).

11. **Step Eleven:**

Tag People, Locations, and use Sharing Options.

Before you press the blue "Share" button in the top right corner, there's a few more tiny features you can add to the post.

The first option is to "Add Location". If you click it, you can search for the location you want to assign to the image and Instagram will tag it along with the post. I find this especially useful if you're taking a picture in a memorable location, like a view from the Empire State Building or scuba diving off of the Galapagos.

It can also be great for showcasing restaurants, bars, or events that you wish to link the image to. In this way, adding locations can be a helpful tool in a variety of promotional strategies, or simply to add more context to a post. People often like to know where a post is happening. Using location tags can potentially lead to more likes and follows.

The second option is to "Tag People". You could do this to tag people shown in the image, credit an artist who contributed, credit the original poster, or even to get the attention of accounts who might have an interest in the post, especially the large curators who might re-post you on their account. This can lead to a massive boost of followers.

When it comes to tagging large accounts, such as a curator of travel photos that has millions of followers, be aware of their "rules". When you check out their page, many have the necessary qualifications in their bio about how to get re-posted on their page. Besides tagging them, you may need to also follow them and comment on something in their page. It varies per account, but the reward is worth doing the research.

All you have to do is click the "Tag People" button, and then click on anyone/anywhere in the image to add a tag. You search for the specific username, and then can drag the tag around the image to put it in the right location. Just don't over-tag. Posts with 20 tags on them seem desperate and ruin the aesthetic.

I actually tag my own account, *"poem_wars"*, in my posts, in addition to tagging the creator of the post. It's hard to track the metrics on tagging yourself to see if doing so actually makes a difference. However, my rationale is that when you see a post, and then tap on the pic, any tags attached will pop up. So, if your own profile is tagged, it's just another way to bring people to your page.

Even if it's only 3 or 4 or 10 people, that might bring in a few more followers. And although it's "only" a few, every follower counts. Your following is a collection of individual followers. Never forget that.

The third option is to share the post on another social network. Instagram gives you the option of sharing to your Facebook page, Twitter, or Tumblr. I personally don't use these very often because I predominantly focus on my Instagram following.

However, most people utilize a variety of social media for their brand, art, and overall following, so connecting those accounts to Instagram and sharing your posts is an easy way to increase the pure volume of content you are sharing with your audience.

You can easily connect these different social media accounts in Instagram's menu options.

12. **Step Twelve:**

Press "Share"!

Holy cow, Batman! We've posted! We did it! Let the follows and likes roll in! We're famous!

Not exactly. Yet.

This is the tedious part. Not the hard part, but the tedious part.

Also, it's extremely simple. A chimpanzee could do it. No joke. It requires hitting the same few buttons over and over again.

But if you want likes and followers and fame and fortune, you need to do this - unless you own a chimpanzee, in which case go have a beer and let him take the reigns.

On a more serious note: <u>This may be the the most important step of anything I describe in this book.</u>

Why?

Because this is where your account goes from largely unnoticed to very noticeable. And once you have eyes on you, likes roll in, then followers, then more eyes, likes, and followers until you've generated some serious force.

Creating this type of momentum will only take a week, maybe even less. And it starts here.

This is the simple process, after pressing "Share":

A. Take those hashtags you've collected, <u>all 30</u>, then <u>copy and paste all of them into the first comment of your post</u>.

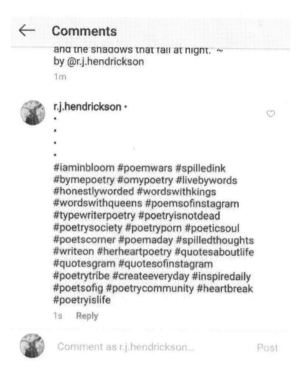

Yes, you're commenting on your own post. Don't worry - this is acceptable Instagram etiquette. Make sure you have your five "dots" (or whatever symbol you choose) over the top, as this will hide your comment under an inconspicuous "..." (mentioned earlier in "The Pivot" section of Part One).

Now, all of these hashtags will be applied to your post, meaning the post will show up under every single individual hashtag page for each of the hashtags you just typed out. They are now visible to far more than just your following.

Next:

B. <u>Click on a hashtag</u>. Ideally it's something that has between 300,000 - 1 million posts in it, one of the larger ones you've selected in your 30.

This is <u>extremely</u> strategic. You're about to be liking and following a LOT of people, and the hashtags that have a higher number of posts are being posted at a more frequent rate: every 20 or 30 seconds there will be a new post. *#spilledink*, *#bymepoetry*, and *#poetrycommunity* are all good examples in my specific niche.

Once you are under this tag, you'll see the page separated into two sections - "Top Posts" and "Recent Posts". <u>Go to the "Recent Posts" section</u>.

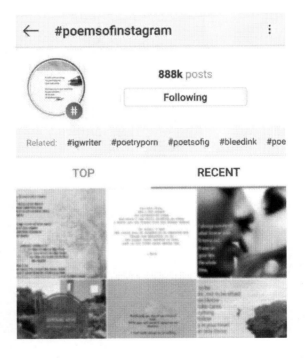

Now we begin.

C. <u>Click on one of the posts</u> at the very top of the gallery queue. This will bring you out of the gallery view into a list view where each post is large, front and center. You can scroll down this list to see all the posts recently posted. The newest will be at the top, with older ones the farther as you scroll down. Now, <u>double tap the post to "like," and click the little blue "follow" button next to their username to follow them</u>.

Scroll down and do it again to the post underneath. And again. And again. Aim to do it to 20-30 posts. You don't have to like and follow every person. Over time, you'll find that many people who post are accounts you already follow.

You can still like their posts and move on. Liking posts reminds people that you exist, and will cause them to visit your profile, like your posts, and follow you if they don't already.

Feel free not to follow anyone who doesn't seem to fit in your niche, or posts something you don't connect with. Feel free to not like a post you genuinely don't like. But keep liking and following, scrolling farther and farther down as you do this.

Remember - chimpanzees can do this. You're competing with them if you think this is hard work.

D. After about 20-30 posts, switch to a new hashtag and repeat. Just go back to your own post, click on a new hashtag in your group of 30 with a similar popularity as the one you just used, go to "Recent Posts", and do the exact same process.

The reason we switch once you get about 20-30 posts down is because at that point you're dealing with posts that are maybe 30 minutes to 1 hour old. The point of liking and following recent posts is because these users are both active and have few likes on their posts. If you're the first person or even the 10th person to like their post, it's very likely they'll want to follow you back, especially if you've just followed them as well.

They just posted. They're watching their feed, excited (just like you were, at this same moment) for all of those likes and follows to roll in. Yet unlike you, they aren't hard at work liking and following and rapidly building their community. Instead, they are sitting on their ass, ready to look at the profiles of anyone who showed their posts any ounce of attention.

These are the people who will like your posts, the people who will follow you, the people who will come back repeatedly to like your work again and again. Because they were like-less and had few followers, and you showed them support and encouragement just by engaging with their posts early on.

Do not undervalue these people. These users ARE your Instagram. They comprise almost all of your likes and follows. If you like and follow only the "Top Posts", all of the popular accounts, do you know what will happen?

Nothing.

Because those people could give two shits about you and your hopes and dreams as an Instagrammer. They are already Insta-famous and therefore, largely unsupportive to newbies. You are just another like and follow to them, and they will usually never return the favor.

After liking and following about 20 users per each of the 5 hashtags, you don't have to stop. If you're really driven, keep liking more photos - either within the same hashtags you just visited, or others within your group of 30.

The reason we try to only follow about 100 users is because we don't want to overly bulk up our follower vs. following ratio. On top of that, Instagram can potentially give you a temporary ban for following too many people in a short period of time.

Liking more photos, however, will still bring in more followers. It will bring in less than when you both like and follow, but it still can be worth the extra time.

Why do we have to do this immediately after we post? Why is it critical that we do this in the first few minutes after posting? Can't we just wait and do this at a random time and seem the same results.

These are all good questions.

The answer is that doing this method immediately after posting is the most effective way to amplify the Instagram algorithm, boosting your post beyond its natural reach. Instagram boosts the visibility of posts based on their performance. It evaluates recent posts that are getting a lot of likes and bringing in a lot of followers as a quality, popular post, and therefore will help to increase its visibility.

Liking and following immediately after posting increases the likelihood that your post will perform well out of the gate. In the end, Instagram is a business. They are here to help those who bring in the most user engagement, because that benefits them greatly. Increases their active daily users, brings in new accounts, and allows their platform to grow.

Don't think of the method as just "hacking" the system. It is benefiting everyone on the platform. Instagram gets more engagement through your effort. Those you like and follow build up their page. And, in turn, you are rewarded with more visibility and a greater audience.

It's a win-win-win. The obvious choices in life come from analyzing what will bring the greatest benefit to the most people. If you can help yourself while helping others, pull the trigger and take action. The force of your efforts will be amplified by the sheer value you are putting into the world.

Don't be a martyr. You deserve to thrive.

Passing the Finish Line

So - you've done 20 likes and follows (at least) per hashtag for 5 different relevant hashtags with active users, and potentially liked a handful of photos on top of that. Congratulations! You've just done your daily workout and can sit back, relax, and enjoy the fruits of your labors.

And, oh boy, does it feel good. The result will be sudden and astounding. Likes and follows start to roll in like a rising tide. If you've previously been posting without hashtags, liking and following nobody, you will suddenly double, triple, even quadruple the likes and follows you've gotten before.

The best part is: this will only grow. With every new post, with every like and follow you give, the more you will receive. Why? Because you are gaining more clout. You have more and more followers. Your posts have more and more likes. You're on your way to Insta-fame.

You might be wondering - as you like and follow more and more people with each post, won't you eventually be following a massive amount of accounts?

The short answer: yes.

Luckily, there are great ways to keep your following to follower ratio in check, all of which will be covered in detail in Part 3. You can easily slim down the amount of accounts you are following to make your account look less desperate and more in-demand using apps that will help you unfollow many users at a time - people who don't follow you back, or accounts that followed and then immediately unfollowed you.

However, as you reach a large enough size, about 5,000-7,500 followers or so, you can transition past the follow method (if you'd like to, although it's not necessary). Ideally, you have also been slimming down your ratio to the point where you only follow about 1,000 accounts or less by manually unfollowing or using unfollowing apps (covered in Part 3). You can now relax and refine your strategy.

Rather than constantly follow new accounts, you can begin to entertain the options, detailed below.

Option #1: <u>Post and Like Posts</u>

After each post, simply proceed with "the method", above. Stay in the recent post section, just as you have been doing. However, rather than liking AND following accounts, simply <u>just like their posts</u>.

Because both liking and following has a higher probability of those accounts following you back, you're going to need to like more photos to get the same result. Whereas before you followed/liked 20 posts for 5 separate hashtags, now you'll need to like 50 posts per each of the 5 hashtags.

This seems like a lot of work, but it takes no more time than liking/following. You're no longer clicking that little "follow" button, allowing you to scroll through posts and like them at a much faster rate.

I started experimenting with this strategy when I had about 6,000 followers. I simply made a post and then did nothing. By the next day, I had pulled in approximately 20 followers simply by posting. After multiple repetitions of just posting, obtaining similar results, I posted *and* liked about 50 posts in 5 different hashtags, sticking to the recent posts section.

Doing so brought in about 40-50 followers per post, and no change in the amount of likes on my posts. In fact, one of those posts was a jackpot, bringing in over 1,750 likes. Clearly, this method can be as effective as the like/follow method, albeit liking/following consistently brings in the most followers, every time.

This method appears to only achieve similar results once your account has a substantial amount of users, perhaps because your account seems to have notoriety and therefore the audience thinks it is worth following. It is less effective for younger accounts.

Of course, the more posts I liked, the more followed accounts followed back. It's up to you how much time you'd like to invest. However, this is an easy option for increasing your following without increasing the amount of accounts you follow, thus bettering your follower-to-following ratio day after day.

Option #2: <u>Post More Posts</u>

This strategy is a good alternative for some people. If you are posting once a day, post twice. Logically, this should double the amount of accounts that follow you per day, given the posts are of consistent quality.

I again tested this when I had about 6,000 followers. When I just posted twice a day, I organically pulled in about 40-50 followers per day. While it took more time to post twice, that time was offset by the amount of time I saved by not having to follow and like accounts. This is a great option if you love posting but hate liking and following after each post.

As with Option #1, it will preserve your slim follower-to-following ratio. However, it is also only effective once you have already amassed a substantial following, and will likely yield less results than actively following and/or liking accounts as well.

Option #3: Post More AND Like Posts

This is the most time consuming option, but it has the most substantial effect. Doing so combines the effectiveness of both of the above options, and more or less guarantees that you will bring in 2,000 followers a month at the very least.

Testing this option yielded beautiful results. I would make two posts per day, and then like 50 posts per 5 hashtags. This daily investment brought in a minimum of 30 followers per post, and often 80-100 or so followers per day. While nothing is as effective as liking and following after every post, this combination of alternative options yields great results and allows you to no longer worry about constantly having to unfollow stale accounts every few days.

Use whichever option fits best, however keep it consistent. Persist, and you will continue to see steady results.

At this stage of the game, you'll be blown away by the wave of enthusiasm and engagement coming from your audience. It's a great feeling, watching your following grow and grow with unstoppable force. People will comment. They'll tag you. They'll DM you and compliment you on your work.

You may be asking - does it ever get easier? When does all of this effort and persistence pay off?

I have some good news for you:

Once you hit 10,000 followers, **everything** changes.

Shortly before publishing this book, I discovered the beautiful truth. Once you hit 10k followers, Instagram changes their algorithm for you. Your posts get double the engagement. You get double the likes and double the follows. Your reach becomes massive.

I can only assume that this is Instagram's reward for all of your work building a following. They bookmark your account as important, an account that will bring them more active users on the platform and therefore make them more money.

The algorithm is still a mystery, and in the "Follower to Following Ratio" section of Part Three, I'll explain more about these particular benchmarks based on the metrics from "Insights" and my general observations. The algorithm changes each time you hit certain numbers of followers. These numbers become goals for you on this journey. They become targets you can use to motivate yourself to keep persisting, to get to the next step.

Once you hit 10,000 followers, something changes. Perhaps it is public perception. Perhaps it is the algorithm. Whatever the cause, it feels glorious.

This is something you deserve.

This is something you created for yourself.

Follow

Part 3

The

Aftermath

Refining and Building

You're seeing progress. You're seeing your following grow, getting more and more engagement. You're in a rhythm of repeating the posting process and making it a habit.

Now what?

Now, we need to refine and polish, to tweak, to take what works and make it even better. This is the truly exciting part. We're now able to move past the initial hurdles and onto a quest for perfection.

This is a chance to understand the identity of our page, make higher quality posts, and better engage our following. We can seek out bigger and better opportunities on the Instagram platform. Our brand will take shape, finding a solid, unshakeable foothold in the larger Instagram community.

We also need to eliminate anything that is holding us back.

We're now following too many people and need to slim down, to improve our follower to following ratio. There's a fix for that. We have hashtags that aren't performing as well as others. There's a fix for that too. We have too many DM's, or have inconsistent amounts of likes and follows depending on the type of post, or are having a hard time figuring out the best time to post. There are fixes for all of these problems. Let's cut the fat.

In order to best target the many facets of the refinement process, I'm going to break it down into the following categories, and we can tackle each one until your page is a glowing hub of activity, a polished statue of Instagram magnificence.

Here are your Instagram ABC's.

The ABC's

A. Creating a Business Profile

B. Post Frequency

C. Refining Hashtags

D. Follower to Following Ratio

E. Unfollowing

F. Comments

G. Direct Messages

H. Refining Posts

I. 3rd Part Apps

J. Utilizing the Story, Live Video, and Links

K. Paid Advertising

L. Paid Likes and Followers

While these ABC's are largely comprehensive, many of these topics probably warrant their own book. Each are worth exploring in depth. For now, I just want to give you the basic tools and information necessary to properly address each topic, and from there you can experiment, research, and explore other sources and resources.

The goal of this chapter is to take the fuel we created in the last chapter - the posting process - and use it more efficiently and effectively to accelerate your page and explore new heights. Even if you just lightly address each of the following tweaks, refinements, course corrections and damage controls, you will greatly increase the quality, health, and size of your Instagram page.

This is the difference between 500 followers per month versus 2,000 followers per month. Use this advice wisely.

However: don't get too distracted by the big picture and forget to keep posting.

Every.

Damn.

Day.

(Persist)

A. Creating a Business Profile

Instagram allows you to turn your page into a business profile. Doing this doesn't change the look of your page, although it does let you add a small sub-category under your title, such as "Publisher", "Musician/Band", or "Public Figure".

The beauty of turning your page into a business profile is that you get access to <u>boatloads</u> of data: you can discover how your posts are performing, the reach of your page, the demographics of your following, and much, much more. Very valuable stuff.

To do this, simply **go to your Instagram profile, click the "settings" button in the top right corner** (the one with the 3 vertical dots).

1085 profile visits in the last 7 days

This will bring you to the settings page.

Then, **scroll down, and click "Switch to Business Account".**

 Settings

Posts You've Liked

Original Photos

Search History

Cellular Data Use

Language

Private Account

When your account is private, only people you approve can see your photos and videos. Your existing followers won't be affected.

Switch to Business Account

It will prompt you to connect to Facebook by choosing a page. If your page doesn't show up on the list, you'll need to create one on Facebook first. If you don't have a Facebook, sign up for Facebook and then create a page.

You get the idea.

Creating a page is simple, and takes less than 5 minutes. Just title it something relevant (I titled my page "Poem Wars"), and you're good to connect.

Alternatively, at the bottom of that prompt on Instagram, beneath "Next", Instagram allows you to create a Facebook page directly through a "skip" link.

Connect to Facebook

Business profiles on Instagram are linked to Facebook Pages and are subject to their **Terms**.

Choose Page　　　　　　　　　　　　　　　>

Just title it, categorize it, and boom: "You've created and a Facebook Page". Confirm your contact details and click <u>done</u>.

Choose categories for your business profile

Select a category and subcategory so people know what your business is about.

Choose a Category

Local Business   Personal Blog   Product/Service   Art   Mu

That's it!

"Welcome, R.J. Hendrickson. Your page 'Poem Wars' has been linked to your business profile. You'll be able to edit it on Facebook. Now, you can get started with new business tools like promotions and insights about your posts and followers."

Thanks, InstaBot!

On your profile page, in the top right corner, you'll see a strange little bar graph symbol. Click that to see insights about your page. You can track your stories, your audience, and create paid promotions through the Instagram platform (more on paid promotion later).

If you click on your individual posts, you can view insights on how each is performing. Unfortunately, these insights are only available on posts made <u>after</u> you created your business profile.

The metrics provided through the business profile are invaluable. They will give you the most comprehensive bird's eye view of your page, and save you hours of time and stress in the refinement process.

Whether you see your page as a business or not, these resources are well worth the 5 minutes it takes to turn your page into a business profile.

Make sure to add this tool to your toolkit as early on as possible.

B. Post Frequency

Making more posts doesn't necessarily equate to more likes and followers. There's a sweet spot that varies for each type of page. You'll have to find yours. Instagram's ever-changing, super-duper-top-secret algorithm seems to reward accounts that post frequently (but not TOO frequently) by giving them more visibility on home pages and in searches.

A good rule of thumb is to make *at least* **1 post per day** but *no more than* **3 posts per day.**

I do one post a day and see a consistent increase in my overall growth: about 50-70 followers a day, on average. Some days are 30 followers, other days are over 100. It varies, but doing more than two posts doesn't seem to have a major effect, at least for the poetry niche. However, posting less than once a day will limit your growth, without a doubt.

The elephant in the room is that creating posts can take a very long time.

With Poem Wars, it is relatively quick because I re-post. I just need to search for a poem that sticks out to me, screenshot, format, crop, write the captions, tag, share, and then post the hashtags. However, if you are taking photos, creating videos, writing your own poetry, painting or designing artwork, or any nature of content creation, posting at least once every day can be a battle.

The key is to have a backlog of posts. Before you even make your first few posts, you should have a handful of upcoming posts lined up so that you don't have to stress out every day trying to create your next one. Stay at least a few days ahead. If you're really on top of it, stay a week ahead.

While you're posting content that you already have in your pocket, you'll have the time to create new content and decide how far in the future you'd like to share it. Sometimes you'll find you want to share immediately. Other instances you'll find that the timing isn't right and that particular post should sit on the back-burner for a while.

Regardless, stay ahead of the game and you'll avoid the stress of feeling like you're constantly pushing back your Instagram posting deadline due to a lack of content.

It seems that for most artists sharing their work on Instagram - writers, graphic designers, painters, musicians - one post a day does the trick. These types of posts usually take the longest to create. However, if you're posting photography oriented posts, more than one post a day might help, as photo posts are quicker to view than writing, for instance, and therefore can be seen in a higher volume.

For accounts that are the most socially oriented - lifestyle pages, actors, models, influencers, bloggers, vloggers, or general social-media-ites who share their lives on the internet every day to a highly engaged audience of fans - all can definitely benefit from 2-3 posts every day, as well as active use of the Instagram story or live-streaming functions.

People want to constantly see what is going on in your life - morning, noon, and night. Such is the nature of those types of accounts. The plus side of this is that you're frequently documenting your day and can churn out rapid content.

Don't overdo it, though. There's a fine line between in-demand and desperate. You want to restrain yourself just enough to keep your audience curious, actively excited to see your next post, but not overloaded with too much *you-ness*. Too many posts and your account will overwhelm them. Not enough, and they'll forget you exist.

There's far too much content on social media, and we all have short attention spans. Thus,

Irrelevancy = Death

If you post daily, and continue the like/follow method, or post/like method, your audience will continue to grow.

I promise.

C. Refining Hashtags

Over time, you may realize that some of your hashtags contain posts that are irrelevant to your niche, or simply lack posts in general.

Delete each dud and find more relevant ones. Still, try to always stay at 30. Eventually, as you grow, you'll start hitting the "Top Post" section in a lot of your hashtags. This will only increase your visibility (as well as give you some considerable street cred). At one point, I realized that my Poem Wars posts were in the top 5 posts in over 22 of my 30 hashtags. Pretty insane - but not unrealistic.

All it takes is strategic use of appropriate hashtags to get to that level. Currently, every other post or so I make will reach the Top Post section in a handful of my hashtags simply because I have a large following and an engaged audience. More followers and engagement makes for more visibility, which in turn brings in more followers and engagement. It's always win-win.

While your hashtags will bring in less people compared to the tactic of liking and following, they still will bring in a decent handful of new followers and fans. Hashtags reach a constantly refreshing and new audience in high volume. They only help to diversify your following and let it spread outward like a (happy) virus.

Additionally, liking and following under a new hashtag can bring in a wave of new followers that have never seen your account before, which perhaps opens your page up to a completely different niche - these aren't accounts that frequent your usual hashtag watering holes.

Don't get lazy or arrogant - keep your list updated. Every like and follower counts.

D.   Follower to Following Ratio

I know what you're thinking.

"But but but if we keep following more and more people, post after post, won't we eventually be following wayyyyyy too many people??"

Yes. You will. You will be following a boatload of people, and eventually you're going to have to throw some overboard. Where to start? **Not all of these people will be following you.** At first, this means a pretty skewed ratio in the direction of desperation versus one of prestige. This usually means you are following far more than are following you.

At the start, this is okay. In fact - it can be necessary. For every 5 likes and follows, you'll get about 1 follow back, on average. This rate increases over time, but it's not great at first. You'll have to go into the negative a bit to gain your first 300 or so followers, although there are ways you can recover your ratio very quickly, which I'll address over the following pages.

Once you bypass the 2,000 followers mark, it will get much easier, and you'll find that your effort has a greater return. Perhaps this has to do with the mysterious Instagram algorithm, or perhaps it is just human psychology: people think you must be worth following if 2,000 other people feel that way too. The herd mentality often works to your advantage.

Yet, when you're starting out, you are pushing uphill. The best thing to do is to momentarily suspend your ego, and just play the volume game.

Like follow like follow like follow.

Don't worry about your ratio, and don't worry about the results. If you're posting every day, and liking/following about 80-100 people every day, you'll probably build a following of 100-200 people within a week (given you're starting with less than 100 followers). You'll be following about 500-700 people, unless you've been unfollowing your non-followers every day to preserve a tight ratio. This is a great place to be after only one week.

It's important to note: it will be <u>very</u> difficult to pull in 2,000 followers your first month if you're starting at 0. As noted, the threshold where it's possible, even likely, to gain followers at this rate is when you hit about 2,000.

If you're persistent and disciplined, you can certainly get 2,000 in your first month. If you're slightly less persistent and disciplined, two months is more than enough time to reach this mark.

Once you pass the threshold, however, gaining 2,000 followers a month or more is absolutely realistic. Eventually, you'll be able to phase out of constantly following accounts after each post and can apply other strategies, such as just liking recent posts instead. Those methods are most effective once you hit over 5,000-7,500 followers, which often comes shockingly fast after you get over this first hump. So, when starting out, your primary goal should be to hit the 2,000 mark.

As I mentioned earlier, 10,000 followers is a huge game-changer. This isn't the only level where things get easier though. There are certain benchmarks that will activate the next "stage" of the Instagram algorithm and push you forward at a faster and faster level.

From my observations, these come in about 6 stages:

1. **500** followers

2. **1,000** followers

3. **2,000** followers

4. **4,000** followers

5. **7,500** followers

6. **10,000** followers

This is mostly observed in reach (how many people see your account), likes, comments, and the flow of organic followers that come in every day. You'll see 50-100 likes suddenly turn in 200, then 350, then 500, then 800, then 1,000-2,000 as you hit these marks.

I don't know the next benchmark after 10,000 followers. Hopefully, I'll be observing that in the coming few months. Yet I can certainly tell you the jump that happens as you pass into the 10k range by comparing my last pre-10k post to my first post-10k post.

The post wasn't any different than my typical posts. It was a similar style, and I used the method of liking about 250 photos within a set of different hashtags after posting. Nothing was done differently, but the effect was substantial. Drastic. Nearly unbelievable.

My post before I hit 10k followers was a solid performer. Here are that post's "Insights":

This is the post I made immediately after hitting 10k followers:

The likes aren't necessarily through the roof. I had made posts that hit that many likes for months, albeit intermittently.

The truly shocking metrics are the Profile Visits, the Follows, the Comments, the Reach, and the Impressions.

14 vs. 36 people commented.

132 vs. 727 people favorited the post.

785 people visited my profile because of the post, vs. the previous post's 44.

184 people followed me directly through the post just for posting, vs. 5 (although the 5 follower post brought in another 60 or so followers through the use of my method).

Overall, the second post alone brought in over 220 total followers just through posting, not including the other ones brought in through my method.

As for the Reach and Impressions, they were astronomical. This post was viewed by over 40,000 Instagrammers, vs. only 6,000 or so.

Obviously, after 10k followers, Instagram seems to boost your posts like crazy. Once there, you have entered the promised land, the land of milk and honey. You are on the fast track. As I said before, everything gets easier.

It's beautiful.

Ok - back to our ratio.

At the end of week one, we can start to groom the ratio - if you haven't already started the process. If you are following

500 people and 100 are following you, you've done your homework, and you're ready to slim down and beautify. Manually unfollowing accounts on Instagram is pure torture. More importantly, it's near impossible to tell if the account your are unfollowing is following you back or not. Don't even try. Save yourself the headache, and rely on some outside help.

There's a plethora of apps that will attach to your Instagram (you sign in and connect to it through the app) and will show you an assortment of information about your following. <u>The most important function is finding the accounts you follow that don't follow you back</u>.

Almost all of these apps will have a function where you can manually unfollow these non-followers with just the click of a button. Some - the ones you want to use - allow you to unfollow blocks of people, sometimes 20-50 at a time. This not only will improve your ratio dramatically, but is also a HUGE time-saver.

A word of warning: <u>Be careful with these apps</u>.

For one, sometimes they give you the wrong info. Some of the people that the app says don't follow you back actually *do* follow you. Make sure you check that the app is accurate before you use it (I'll include some of the apps I've found to be most effective in the "Tools" section at the end of the book).

You can test the accuracy of the app simply by searching for the Instagram profiles that the app deems don't follow you in your own "followers" list (the one on your own page). If the specific username shows up under your "followers" list, but the unfollow app says they don't follow you, then the app lies. Don't use it. Delete it and find a new one.

Found a good one? It's accurate, and you're ready to use it? On to the next step.

E. Unfollowing

Here's why we want to unfollow people who don't follow us back:

A. It improves your follower to following ratio very quickly, and

B. These people can't unfollow you once you unfollow them, because they never followed you in the first place.

All they can do is pout that they lost a follower.

If you unfollow a bunch of people who follow you, many will eventually notice at some point and will unfollow you out of resentment or a sense or rejection. If you do this technique, blindly unfollowing people indiscriminately, <u>your following will drop like flies</u>.

"But but but," you say, *"If I only unfollow these people, won't I still be following 100 people? The ones who are following me - won't my ratio just end up 100 followers and 100 following?"*

Of course not.

It's possible, but extremely unlikely. Think about it. You don't follow every person who follows you. It's just the same as the people you just booted - you followed them, but they didn't follow you back. Likewise, you probably don't follow a solid portion of your Instagram family back.

Make sense?

No?

I know - I've just used some variation of the word "follow" about half a million times. And yes, that's the name of the book, and for good reason. But this is something we need to get right.

I'll simplify.

Let's divide our followers and following into 3 separate categories.

1. **Friends**: These are <u>people you follow who also follow you back</u>. How heartwarming.

2. **Fans**: These are <u>people who follow you that you don't follow back</u>. You cold heartless monster, you.

3. **Assholes**: These are <u>people who you follow that don't follow you back</u>. And they are aptly named.

Now let's take these categories and put them into action with this highly educational example:

Your follower to following ratio is not good - you have 3 followers and follow 4 people. **3 to 4, followers vs. following**. You follow Jill, Bob, Alice, and Sebastian. Jill and Bob both follow you back, meaning they are your **<u>friends</u>**. Alice and Sebastian don't. They're **<u>assholes</u>**.

Using a third party app, you unfollow Alice and Sebastian, who obviously don't appreciate the utter genius of your page.

With those two gone, you now have 3 followers and follow 2 people. **3 to 2, followers vs. following**.

Wait… Jill and Bob follow you, but who is this mysterious 3rd follower? Who is giving you a "net-positive" ratio - a higher number of followers than people you are following? You look, and see that it is some dude named SlinkyMaster808. Who the hell is he?

Answer: who cares?

This is an example of a **fan**. They are people who follow you despite your indifference to their existence. In this situation, YOU get to be the asshole, and not follow them back. Thanks to poor SlinkyMaster808, you get to have a beautiful net-positive ratio of **3 to 2**.

Yes. You're now famous.

If you do maintenance like this once or twice a week, or even a little every other day, you'll always have a good ratio. Instagram limits the amount of accounts you can follow to 7,500, so once 7,500 people follow you, you'll permanently have a net-positive ratio, always having more following you than you could possibly follow.

Bring out the champagne.

Over time, more and more accounts who you have never seen or heard of and definitely never followed will begin to follow you. *Woo! Fans!* Your ratio will get better and better with little to no effort. This is is a simple and wonderful effect of slowly becoming Insta-famous. Bring out more champagne.

Even better - the more followers you have, the more followers you'll get. It's like having your cake, and eating it too, and then getting more cake just for eating the cake you already ate.

You may not want to max out at 7,500 followers. You probably want to have a far lower number. Or simply, you may be wondering what happens once you hit that point. What if you follow every single one of 7,500 accounts that follow you? How can we keep doing the methods at this point? Or, what if you only follow 500-1,000, but don't want to follow anybody else?

Remember: the "method" is simply about increasing visibility. So, you can still post and do the method, however instead of liking/following accounts, instead you'll just be liking accounts, as covered in Step 13, "Passing the Finish Line".

It's important to note, again, that less people will follow you for just liking their posts than if you like their post AND follow them.

This means that you will have to like more posts than you did before with the regular like/follow method. So, if you liked/followed 100 posts and accounts after every time you posted, you might have to now like 200-300 posts.

Same as before, you just pick one of your hashtags, go to "Recent Posts", and go down the list liking post after post.

Luckily, you have two things working for you:

A. You now have a LOT of followers. So when you like someone's posts, especially a newbie, they're going to want to follow you. After all, you're a big account, and they'll want to have more attention from you. For this reason, your conversion rate will be much higher than when you started.

B. Liking is easier and faster than liking AND following every post. You can go rapid fire, so the 200-300 likes will go just as fast as the liking/following method. It might even be fast enough that you can do more than 200-300 total.

Another option, besides simply posting more, is to start commenting more (I will cover this more in depth in the next section). Of course, this takes a lot more time, although it does have a good conversion rate. People often follow those who comment on their posts.

Find what works for you but stick to it. The most important part, at this stage, is to just keep posting. With a larger following, frequent posts, and the proper use of hashtags, your following will continue to grow and grow.

F. Comments

What could comments possibly have to do with growing your page?

Well, they're another powerful tool in your arsenal. Just by commenting on a post, you can gain a follower, likes, or comments back on your own posts. Combine that comment with a like and/or a follow, you greatly increase your chances of getting followed by that user. It's the perfect one-two-punch. I've heard from multiple sources that there is almost a 50% chance that a like/follow/comment combo will result in a follow back.

Another huge benefit of comments is that they can help you connect on a deeper level with your audience. They are a direct, public conversation. People who comment on your posts <u>love</u> getting a reply, and others <u>love</u> seeing that you reply to your fans. "Maybe, *just maybe*, s/he's a good person!" they think. And that hope, whether realistic or not, will keep them coming back to like your posts and send you endless heart emoji DM's.

The best Instagrammers use comments to their benefit. I don't often comment when I am liking and/or following after I post ("the method"), mainly because it would take significantly more time. However, perhaps not doing so is missing the opportunity to utilize a precious resource. The jury is out.

If it appeals to you, or works for you, make it an active part of your arsenal. While the goal of this book is to set you up for success, every hypothesis must be proven to become a theory, and every theory must be challenged to stand the test of time. So, keep experimenting and your page will only continue to evolve and grow.

G. Direct Messages (DM's)

Direct messages, or "DM's", are another sacred Instagram resource.

Think about it. DM's open up the opportunity for you to message ANYONE on Instagram - including people who don't follow you - and immediately initiate a conversation. Moreover, your audience can message you, not only to give you feedback and compliments, but to even provide you with opportunities for promotion and financial gain.

I've personally used DM's to start conversations with the founders of pages that have 50k+ followers, to cross-promote my page with other Instagrammers, and to run entire poetry submission campaigns. They work. The glory days of email are gone. Responses to DM's are rapid, even immediate, and it is much easier to initiate and continue a conversation than other forms of communication.

Direct messages allow you to create a personal relationship with the users you are trying to start a dialogue with. I've received DM's with more than just poetry submissions. People will reach out asking for advice, or simply to express gratitude for the existence of my page.

I used to avoid answering them; naturally, there will be a handful of spam in your inbox. However, once I started connecting with people in short, direct conversations, I started making countless bonds with audience members who went on to be my biggest, most highly-engaged fans.

Don't miss out on the power of DM's to deepen bonds with potential customers and audience members. It will bring both closer to your page. In the end, if a simple one-minute conversation can create a lifetime fan, why waste the opportunity? Even though you will never meet 99.999% of the people you talk to, social media exists to connect us in a way that was never before possible on the internet.

To open up your Direct Messages, just click the little blue arrow button in the top right corner of your homepage, the one with the numeric messages bubble attached to it.

From there, you will be able to access all of the messages in your inbox, allowing you to initiate conversations, send pictures, share your Instagram story, and more.

H. Refining Posts

This is another topic that requires its own book. However, refining posts is a simple strategy if you utilize metrics - the insights offered by Instagram.

To start, keep upping the quality of your posts: better quality photos, writing, models, fashion, videos, so on and so forth. Keep perfecting. Most importantly, notice <u>what works</u>. Sometimes what *you* like isn't exactly what your *audience* likes. Literally, what they <u>like</u>: start with your posts that have the most likes. The most comments. The posts that seem to bring in the most followers after posting. Your audience has preferences, and you have to balance their taste with your own to maximize the growth of your page.

Looking at Instagram's "Insights" will provide further information on what's been working. Click "View Insights" underneath your posts and you'll be able to see how many users viewed your profile after seeing your post, the amount of people who marked your post as a favorite, how many followed you after seeing it, as well as the reach and amount of impressions the post drew in. It's an incredibly valuable resource.

For instance, I had a post that received over 1,950 likes, 15 comments, was favorite by 415 people, brought in more than 120 profile visits, reached 19,100+ accounts, and had 22,700+ impressions. The post alone brought in over 40 followers (this didn't even include what I brought in from using my method after posting). A surprising 1,800 impressions came from just the hashtags.

Don't doubt the power of hashtags, even if you already have a lot of followers! 86% of the accounts reached weren't already following me, while only 300 of the impressions came from people already viewing my profile. What this means is that the post brought in a lot of new users who maybe had never seen my page before.

[*For reference*: "Reach" is the number of unique accounts that have seen a specific post, while "Impressions" are the total number of times your post has been seen (which includes multiple viewings).]

Another valuable resource is the more comprehensive Insights available on your main page. If you go to your profile and click the bar graph in the top right corner, you can see activity over the course of the week under the "Activity" tab, posts ranked by their impressions under the "Content" tab, and information about your audience under the "Audience" tab.

The "Audience" tab is a gold mine. It will tell you what cities and countries your audience is from, their age range, gender, and which days and times bring in the most followers. Learn your audience and your posts will get better and better. Your engagement will rapidly rise.

Knowing the times of day that you are getting the most followers is critical information. This will give you an idea of the best times to post in order to maximize your following. Also, knowing the location of your audience will further help you with timing posts, as it will inform you of what time-zone your audience is in when seeing posts.

For instance, I have a very large audience from India. Because they are 9.5 hours ahead of my time-zone, I know that posting late in the evening will hit all of my audience at once. If I post at 11pm in Boston, it will be 8pm on the North American west coast, the morning in India, and even later in eastern Asia. Posting at around this time means more likes, more follows, and more comments.

If you aren't getting as much engagement as you think you should be, or the results are erratic, post-time metrics will help you figure out the best routine to maximize your engagement. Timing really does make a difference, so experiment to learn what works best, and then stick to those times. It will soon become habit, just like eating dinner or sleeping.

Take these metrics and use them. Refine your next post to be stylistically similar to those posts that have received the best engagement. Focus on similar content, content that fits in with your greatest hits but also expands the quality of any outliers.

Keep each post true to yourself, but let your audience also have a say. In the end, we are trying to have growth and impact, and these numbers will be a huge help in guiding you toward these goals.

To access your Insights, click the bar graph symbol at the top of your profile page.

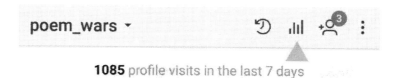

1085 profile visits in the last 7 days

This will bring you to your account's Insights page.

To see the insights on a particular post, click "View Insights" under the post itself.

This will bring you to your post's Insights page.

I. 3rd Party Apps

I've mentioned 3rd party apps a few times in previous chapters. At the end of this book, in the "Tools" section, I'll detail the specific ones I've used and find most effective.

While Instagram apps come and go frequently, either due to Instagram's strict guidelines or perhaps failures on the part of the app's developers, there are 3 primary types that will help you grow your Instagram:

1. Design Apps

2. Planning Apps

3. Follow/Unfollow Apps

I'll describe the purpose of each, both the benefits and the drawbacks.

1. Design Apps

These are applications that will allow you to greatly enhance the quality of your posts, including a vast variety of filters, fonts, and photo-editing tools that aren't available on Instagram's photo-editor. Many include stickers, facial smoothing tools, backgrounds, framing, selective spot removal tools, and much, much, much more.

These apps can easily be found in the app stores for both Apple and Android. A simple search for "photo editing", "Instagram editor", "photo filter", or "photo design" should bring up a plethora of options. Choose the ones that have the features that suit your needs.

It might take a little trial and error to figure out the one you like the best, but once you use them effectively and find the ones that best helps you accomplish your desired post style, stick with them. Using the same app, same fonts, and same type of editing will help to create consistency between your posts.

These apps are usually free, but some have premium options with enhanced capabilities for a small purchase price. Personally, I've done fine just using the free ones. Don't go overboard with post design. Just use the tools you need to make the post you need.

Sometimes having more editing options can over-complicate things and bring out your (evil) inner perfectionist. Simple tends to be better. That being said, don't neglect using these apps. All of the best Instagrammers use them to great advantage. They will take your Insta game to the next level.

2. Planning Apps

These applications allow you to organize and schedule posts ahead of time. This means that you have the ability to arrange your posts with more foresight, creating a better aesthetic on your feed, while - more importantly - keeping yourself on a consistent schedule. You'll be well ahead of posting when you have a pre-made plan, so you won't find yourself forgetting to post when daily stress or work obligations pop up, as they always seem to do.

While these apps can't auto-post for you, they'll set reminders that alert you to post, and you can directly insert posts from the app by pressing an in-app link that will bring you (and your post) straight to the Instagram post-creation page. Often, the app will copy your pre-written caption automatically so that you can simply paste it in the Instagram caption box and share. Additionally, these apps will help you create and save hashtags groups so you can use them however you please, alternating between the specific hashtag groups that apply to different types of posts.

I used one of these apps for a while, but I didn't find that it wasn't much more effective for me than just having posts organized on my phone ahead of time. This means that my captions and hashtags were already prepared in my phone's notes, ready to copy and paste, with my photos saved in a post folder.

I just picked the same time of day every day to post, and posting became pure instinct, a habitual and rote process that came without even thinking. However, I only posted once a day, and still do. If you're dealing with more than one post per day, having these apps can be incredibly helpful to keep you on schedule and well prepared.

3. Follow/Unfollow Apps

These applications, while unbelievably valuable, can be pure evil. Many are finicky and potentially dangerous to the health of your account. If the app doesn't work properly, it can cause certain features of your page to be temporarily locked up, or in the worst case even cause your page to be banned. Proceed with caution.

Often these apps allow you to gain followers or likes by watching ads, downloading apps, or liking and following other app users. This builds up "tokens", which can be used to "purchase" likes and follows.

I **highly** recommend you don't use this function.

For one, it is extremely annoying to watch ads and download crappy apps that you are going to immediately delete after. On top of that, it mainly leads to non-organic likes and followers that don't have any real engagement. They'll throw off your metrics, and many of those users will unfollow you in a day or two.

Protect your metrics. They are extremely important.

However, as mentioned earlier, a beautiful feature of most of these apps is that they will show you accounts that follow you that you don't follow back (fans), accounts that you follow that also follow you (friends), accounts that you follow that don't follow you back (assholes), and the people who followed you and then immediately unfollowed you (douchebags).

It is the latter two, the assholes and the douchebags, that we will be unfollowing. As previously described in Section D, make sure the apps are accurate, and that these users <u>actually</u> don't follow you. If you don't do this, you could accidentally lose a lot of followers.

I've done it, and it is painful. But if the app is accurate - and this is the fun part - we can unfollow all of these fine people and <u>greatly</u> improve our ratio.

Most apps will allow you to both batch unfollow accounts (20-50 users at a time) and manually unfollow accounts as well (1 user at a time). These methods each have their pluses and minuses. Batch unfollowing allows you to not have to put in as much effort.

However, if you overuse it, you could get in trouble with the Instagram police. Currently - and don't quote me on this, because it's always changing - Instagram allows you to unfollow about 50 users every half hour. This means, theoretically, you can unfollow around 2,400 accounts every day. That's if you didn't sleep. It's better to not push it, and instead aim to unfollow 50 users or less every hour, maximum.

If the Instagram Gestapo see that you're cheating the system, you may not be able to unfollow (or even follow) accounts for a week or so: a temporary suspension. It has happened to me, and it's extremely annoying. Even worse, it will slow your progress.

Manually unfollowing these accounts on the app is a bit slower and tedious, but ultimately is <u>far</u> better than having to unfollow these same accounts on Instagram. For one, you can unfollow directly through the app. You also have more control, and can "whitelist" any account you don't want to unfollow - for instance, celebrities you like or accounts in your niche that inspire you, even if they don't follow you back. "Whitelisting" them simply means that you keep the app from accidentally unfollowing them. As with the batch unfollow function, manually unfollow no more than 50 accounts an hour to avoid suspension.

Most importantly, using these apps will put all of those non-followers into one list, something you would not be able to see on Instagram. Rather than search from account to account, it's all here. Your time is important.

So, to summarize:

> **Design apps** increase the quality of your posts.
>
> **Planning apps** keep you organized and on schedule.
>
> **Follow/Unfollow apps** improve your follower to following ratio.

Use them to your benefit and quickly see the results.

J. Utilizing the Story, Live Video, and Links

The Instagram Story is an expansive new feature. Not only does it allow you to increase your visibility, but also adds a more immediate, personal way to share and connect with your audience. Posts, while the foundation of Instagram, are static. You make a post and it is preserved there in marble, a permanent feature of your page. It is a foundation, a building block, that creates the whole.

A Story, on the other hand, is transient. It only lasts 24 hours. Like Snapchat, it takes advantage of the feeling of immediacy and intimacy. When you post a Story, not only does your audience have a limited time to view it, but it also hits the top of their homepage. *"Ooh! Something shiny and new! Must click on this."*

People love seeing updates, and when you post a story, they feel like you are more present with them, almost in direct communication. Live videos take this idea to the Nth degree. Your audience can be right there with you, living your life alongside you, seeing your face and hearing your voice, watching you live or sing or dance or converse with them.

This intensifies connection as well as identification between you and you audience. You let them into a vulnerable, intimate part of your life to share an experience with you. You can in real-time respond to their comments, interacting with your following as they express their viewpoints and love for you as you express your viewpoints and love for them.

While not always applicable to every niche or account, stories and live videos add just another layer of quality and value to your account. Poets can use it for live poetry slams or videos of them reciting their work. Musicians can film live shows or performances. Influencers, models, and actors can take you with them on their day to day life.

Personally, I used them to post direct comments, reminders of contests or deadlines, to showcase winning poetry, or create buzz for a new product or campaign. You can throw in # or @ tags to let people click on them and visit others' profiles, bring them to specific hashtags, or (if you have over 10,000 followers) actually let them click direct links to your products, be it books, clothes, accessories, or whatever else you'd like to sell.

As a growth and sales tool, Live Videos and Stories are magic. They are a new and evolving addition to the Instagram platform, so take the time to experiment with them before they become utilized by every account and the competition grows too fierce.

With social media, every new feature is an opportunity to take advantage of, to get ahead of the pack and do something that hasn't been done before. Think outside the box and use the tools at your disposal to mark your place in the Instagram community.

K. Paid Advertising

You can pay Instagram to promote your posts if you have a business profile. The idea is that it mixes your post in with other posts as an advertisement, giving it visibility to a wider audience. To promote, just click the "Promote" button at the top of your profile page, or the blue button underneath one of your posts.

I tried it, paying $5 per day for 5 days, using one well-performing post as my promotion to try to pull people in to my page. As a way to identify its effectiveness, I posted each of those 5 days as well, but didn't do my usual like/follow method. I got a mere 15-20 additional followers a day using the paid advertising, rather than the 50+ a day through my usual method.

Even though this was early on in the life of my account (probably Month 3) and I wasn't getting many organic followers on the days I didn't post, I'd still get a handful, maybe 5-10. So, factoring in these organic follows, it seemed that the Instagram promotion was only bringing in an extra 10 followers a day.

At $5 a day, that meant I was paying about $0.50 per follower. Sound like a good deal? Hell no, especially given the fact that I was getting 5x that amount every day for free. My chimpanzee method was beating Instagram's advertising algorithms, and I was saving money by doing it.

The Method: 1

Instagram: 0

Chimpanzees: Bananas

L. Paid Likes/Followers

Still not convinced that you should save your money and utilize your persistence instead? Here's another cautionary tale.

I decided to experiment with paying for followers (who would ideally like my posts and increase engagement). On Fiverr, a great freelancing and outsourcing app, one of the freelancers claimed she could increase my following by 500 for only $5. AND, the best part: they'd all be organic users. What a deal! It seemed too good to be true!

It was.

The day after I paid - nothing. No new followers, no more likes than usual. I had stayed up late the night before, so I took a nap. When I awoke an hour and a half later, my following had jumped from 3,200 to 5,200.

I started to have a full-blown panic attack.

500 new followers was an okay number to test. However, 2,000 was nearly double my following. For the next few weeks, I dealt with the massive consequences of my $5 mistake. The accounts that she had brought to my page and added to my following were certainly real. And they were foreign. And most only had 1 or 2 posts on their account.

The worst part: they definitely had no interest whatsoever in poetry. Bizhan from Pakistan liked motorcycles. Виктория from Russia liked rabbits and pictures of her in only her underwear. My following - the <u>fake</u> following of 2,000 new followers - began to drop like flies.

My real following stayed, still loyal, but the Bizhan's and the Виктория's obviously hadn't been paid to stay. It seems that the woman on Fiverr who I had purchased from had a very effective technique: get 2,000 to follow, because only 500 would stick around.

The consequence was two weeks of anguish. I was a few months in, with incredible growth, and suddenly I was losing "followers". It didn't matter that my account was suddenly over 5,000. The fact was that I was now a complete fraud. The fact was that my metrics were now fucked. My ratio was utter bullshit. And my already fragile self-respect? Nowhere to be found.

I began to contemplate abandoning Poem Wars altogether. It was the first time I had ever felt that way, and luckily, the only time I've felt that way since.

I had lost faith.

Later, it dawned on me that I hadn't lost faith in the project - I had really just lost faith in myself. What had once been pride in my persistence and integrity had vanished, only to be replaced by anger and apathy. What was the point of continuing? Rather than feeling constant momentum, I was now fighting an uphill battle.

For every 50 followers I gained, I lost 100. The likes never went up. The comments never went up. Down the road I went back and checked the metrics. As it turned out, nothing had really changed: I was still gaining around 50 real, organic followers every day that I stuck to my normal routine of posting and continued my method of liking and following other users. It was hard to do this despite losing almost 100 followers every day, but I guess I was just too stubborn to give it all up so soon.

So, after about two weeks, everything normalized. I began to see my following (finally) <u>increase</u> every day. I breathed a massive sigh of relief.

Looking back over the metrics now, I still gained about 2,000 followers that month, and eventually lost most of the 2,000 fake followers. So - if I had just stuck with my method, and ignored the urge to prematurely boost my following like some insane, drug-induced cocaine high, I would have seen normal growth. I ended up in the *exact* same position I had started from after a month of purchasing all of those fake followers: 5,200.

Luckily, these ones were real.

That $5 almost killed my page. Seeing it decline, or at the very least, seeing it plateau almost ruined me. I almost abandoned ship - not because it wasn't growing, but because that growth was suddenly concealed. It was artificial fertilizer, and had almost caused the flower to die.

Why did I do it? Likely out of insecurity, or perhaps just impatience. It's important to remember that this is a process. And that ordeal has been a constant reminder to <u>trust the process</u>. It worked even when I couldn't see the results. It was there for me even when I delusionally thought I didn't need it anymore. And I'll never lose faith in it again.

The moral of the story, and my word of warning:

Don't. Purchase. Followers.

It's not worth the psychological toll, and it will not help your page in the long run. It will certainly hurt it in the short-term. Organic growth is something you can see every day. And there's a pride in knowing it is growing because of you.

Looking Forward

You've hit your benchmarks, You got past the daily battle of reaching 2,000 followers and are suddenly seeing rapid growth - growth beyond what you ever thought possible. 50, 60, 70 followers every post, every day. 100's of likes rolling in, including the random outlier that hits the Top Post section of a hashtag and brings in a surge of new followers. You are full of positivity and excitement, seeing limitless possibilities and inspiration everywhere you look.

Take another deep breath.

This is what success feels like. What winning tastes like. Get used to it, but don't succumb to it, because this is exactly the moment we start getting arrogant and lazy.

Examples:

"I don't have to post EVERY day, right? I already have a huge following… What does it matter if I take a day off?"

or,

"I posted, but do I REALLY have to go like and follow a bunch of people? Followers are rolling in while I sleep! I don't need to seem desperate anymore and try to prove myself by following a bunch of peasants."

or,

"I'm a fucking boss. 4,000 followers? None of my friends have 4,000 followers. Even if I stopped trying I'd still be WAY more Insta-famous than they are."

Yes. I'm sure you would be, you Insta-badass. And I'm also sure the minute you flew home from your little ego-vacation you'd notice that followers and likes mean very, very little.

"WHAT? But... Isn't that what this <u>entire</u> book about?! Getting more likes and followers??!!"

Well-

A. I'm glad you've gotten this far. And,

B. Yes, that <u>is</u> what this book is about, but not likes for likes' sake or followers for followers' sake. Like I said, you could just purchase those.

Likes and followers are a metaphor - a representation - for something much larger and far more important:

Connection.

Whether we realize it or not, we are all on Instagram to connect with people. When someone likes one of our selfies, they are giving us a silent, "I like you." When they like our poem, or a picture we took of the Cliffs of Moher, they are saying, "What you've just shown me is beautiful." Every follow is a vote for you to do <u>more</u>. They are waiting for you, investing in the future of your account to make them smile, or laugh, or cry. They are hoping for you to make their day better, whether it is a bad day or not.

We login to Instagram, we like and follow and DM and post because we want to be heard. We want people to hear <u>us</u>. We want to love and be loved, to connect and feel connected to.

I've talked to people on the verge of suicide who found a reason to live because of the community support on Instagram - because they could share themselves and feel accepted. I've found people who have used the app to overcome their depression and self-hatred and insecurity and trauma and loneliness. I've listened to people share their success stories, how this platform helped them publish a best-selling book or how it helped them launch a successful Kombucha company. I've talked to people who have had nobody to talk to, and to people who have had everyone to talk to and no one to listen.

Set your sights low, or set your sights high. But as you grow a following, you will gain a deeper sense of who you really are. You will begin to define your tastes, to decipher your values and determine your dreams.

You will begin to find the purpose of what you are doing and why you are doing it, and it will guide you forward.

Never forget why you're on here. As you grow 2,000 followers a month, you will experience things you have never experienced before. Power, fame, adoration, selfless love, gratitude, deep humility and honesty, limitless support and understanding, opportunity and potential, and a strange, unshakeable sense of responsibility.

You are responsible to your following. The more notoriety you build, the more power you have. The more power you have, the more your actions have consequences.

I do my best to post poems that are healing, that help people come to terms with their pain, loss, heartbreak, anger, or loneliness. Tomorrow, I could easily post a poem that is not healing. One that causes more hate and division. A "fuck you" poem, an "end it all" poem, a "get even" poem. And many of my following could - not would, but <u>could</u> - take that to heart. Many could let that poem accelerate their emotions of hatred and anger and self-destruction.

Would I see the result? Likely not. Would I feel it? Not directly. But deep down, in your soul, there is a weight to every action you take, and those actions are magnified by those that they affect.

Responsibility.

Even in social media, we need to be responsible. Just as I am giving you the methods to gain a following - to gain power, prestige, and influence - I am responsible for how you use those methods. And, in that exact way, you are responsible to those who look toward you as a voice to listen to, a leader to guide them. Your impact and legacy are not built by the amount of likes you receive or the number of followers you have, but by the amount of good you do for your audience.

Don't undermine your own value. Sometimes a simple sentence can change the course of a person's day. I heard one just the other week:

"You don't have to be unhappy."

A guy at the checkout counter at the grocery store said it to his daughter. And I couldn't stop thinking about it the rest of the day. All of the things I'm unhappy about...do I have to be?

Can't I just change them?

Can't I do what I love and am passionate about instead of doing the things I hate just to scrape by?

Can't I gain a massive following in months rather than wait years, idly hoping that, by chance, someone might see my work?

Can't I decide to place my destiny in my own hands, and accept that I have to the power to live the life that I truly want to live?

I'm choosing to live that life. And you should too.

A life that others might want to follow.

Data

In order to give you an idea of what your growth may look like, I'll include a few charts tracking my Poem Wars account's following and likes over time.

Tracking your growth is a great way to understand what is working and what isn't, as well as give you a little motivation whenever you feel like you've hit a drought or are discouraged by what feels like a lack of progress. Data will show you the truth. If I didn't track my growth during my follower plummet after my paid-followers debacle, I may not have realized my account was still growing at the same rate, and perhaps given up altogether.

To start, below is a general graph detailing the change in the follower rate for Poem Wars using the standard method vs. implementing my current following/liking strategy.

146

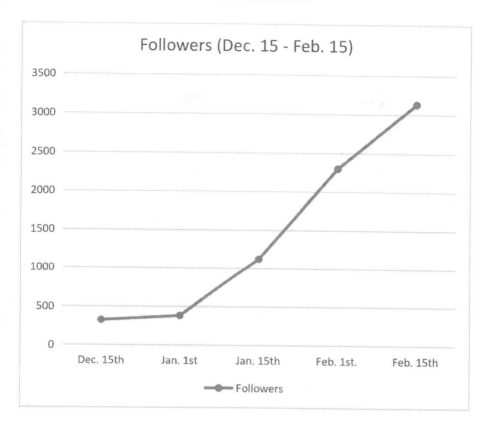

The change of the slope of the line starts in January, upon implementing my strategy, and stays extremely consistent from that point onward.

Below is a table detailing (roughly) my followers per day in this same time period. As you can see, my daily rate of new followers went up significantly as of

January 6th because this is when I started implementing "the method".

Date	Followers	Date	Followers	Date	Followers
Dec. 1	402	17	348	Jan. 1	382
2	394	18	342	2	386
3	393	19	346	3	391
4	392	20	339	4	392
5	401	21	331	5	395
6	388	22	334	6	401
7	396	23	341	7	428
8	402	24	344	8	471
9	387	25	348	9	503
10	374	26	355	10	644
11	372	27	362	11	747
12	358	28	365	12	875
13	344	29	373	13	1001
14	336	30	375	14	1072
16	336	31	381	16	1205

Date	Followers	Date	Followers		
17	1291	Feb 1.	2301		
18	1343	2	2353		
19	1402	3	2404		
20	1489	4	2486		
21	1599	5	2541		
22	1647	6	2601		
23	1738	7	2652		
24	1802	8	2706		
25	1860	9	2728		
26	1912	10	2745		
27	2019	11	2804		
28	2061	12	2911		
29	2120	13	3002		
30	2222	14	3031		
31	2282				

As shown, from January 6th to February 6th, a single month, my following had increased by 2,200 followers.

While likes per post fluctuate much more than followers per day, averaging them out over time shows that they are also gaining at a steady rate.

Some posts, of course, have reached well into the thousands - yet these high-performers aren't necessarily the norm. Still, these posts show you the potential of your page, constantly raising the ceiling to beyond what you thought possible.

The graph on the next page generally tracks the progress of likes over the life of the Poem Wars account. The upward slope is only increasing with more and more momentum every day.

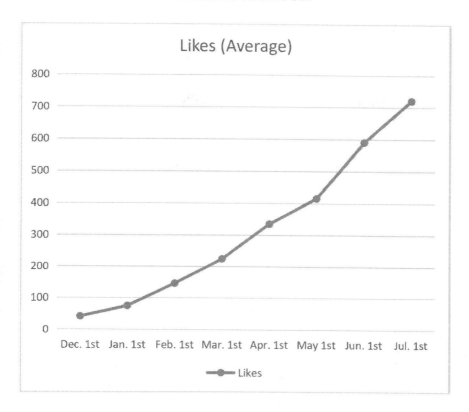

Likes fluctuate frequently, depending upon far too many variables to count. However, it is easy to see the upward trend over time, and tends to be an even better signifier of engagement than even the amount of followers you are gaining every day.

This table shows these likes in more detail, including those high-performing posts that brought in thousands of likes.

Post #	Likes	Post #	Likes	Post #	Likes	Post #	Likes
1	20	21	81	41	811	61	381
2	17	22	87	42	291	62	380
3	31	23	79	43	295	63	361
4	28	24	61	44	250	64	339
5	33	25	67	45	211	65	301
6	48	26	59	46	363	66	885
7	41	27	68	47	264	67	510
8	59	28	86	48	1905	68	304
9	33	29	122	49	518	69	263
10	58	30	130	50	326	70	299
11	47	31	242	51	285	71	310
12	63	32	211	52	332	72	481
13	59	33	244	53	309	73	367
14	35	34	258	54	1649	74	308
15	76	35	315	55	588	75	532
16	68	36	239	56	223	76	250
17	90	37	225	57	890	77	279
18	77	38	851	58	275	78	322
19	74	39	414	59	250	79	221
20	67	40	418	60	579	80	280

81	376	101	448	121	489	141	432
82	234	102	326	122	730	142	478
83	291	103	295	123	563	143	572
84	216	104	1222	124	260	144	393
85	391	105	348	125	250	145	425
86	186	106	400	126	361	146	480
87	257	107	410	127	379	147	595
88	321	108	311	128	557	148	660
89	329	109	390	129	594	149	640
90	207	110	332	130	229	150	778
91	271	111	289	131	1343	151	1837
92	325	112	261	132	513	152	2061
93	216	113	307	133	387	153	942
94	229	114	719	134	310	154	653
95	303	115	358	135	1,086	155	544
96	456	116	367	136	488	156	439
97	193	117	291	137	523	157	1255
98	204	118	294	138	353	158	1433
99	333	119	445	139	841	159	591
100	358	120	554	140	550	160	557

Tools

Here are just a few tools that I've leaned upon, however there are many, many more available for mobile devices, all with a plethora of fantastic features.

Design Apps

1. Photoshop Lightroom CC for Mobile

iOS:

https://itunes.apple.com/us/app/adobe-photoshop-lightroom/id878 783582?mt=8

Android:

https://play.google.com/store/apps/details?id=com.adobe.lrmobile

2. Pixlr

iOS:

https://itunes.apple.com/gb/app/pixlr-photo-editor-for-collages/id 526783584?mt=8

Android:

https://play.google.com/store/apps/details?id=com.pixlr.express&hl =en_GB

3. PhotoDirector

iOS:

https://itunes.apple.com/us/app/photodirector-photo-editor/id907366587?mt=8

Android:

https://play.google.com/store/apps/details?id=com.cyberlink.photodirector&hl=en_US

<u>Planning Apps</u>

1. Preview

iOS:

https://itunes.apple.com/us/app/preview-design-for-instagram/id1126609754?mt=8

Android:

https://play.google.com/store/apps/details?id=com.sensio.instapreview&hl=en_US

2. Plann

iOS:

https://itunes.apple.com/us/app/plann-preview-for-instagram/id1106201141?mt=8

Android:

https://play.google.com/store/apps/details?id=com.webhaus.planyo urgramScheduler&hl=en_US

Unfollow Apps

1. Unfollow for Instagram

iOS: Not Available

Android:

https://play.google.com/store/apps/details?id=app.follow.unfollow &hl=en_US

2. Followers Track for Instagram

iOS:

https://itunes.apple.com/us/app/followers-for-instagram/id597077 652?mt=8

Android: Not Available

3. Follow Cop

iOS: Not Available

Android:

https://play.google.com/store/apps/details?id=com.instagram.follo wcop

4. Mass Unfollow for Instagram

iOS:

https://itunes.apple.com/us/app/mass-unfollow-for-instagram/id1218145349?mt=8

Android: Not Available

Books for Inspiration

1. The Artist's Way by Julia Cameron

https://www.amazon.com/Artists-Way-25th-Anniversary/dp/0143129252

2. The $100 Startup by Chris Guillebeau

https://www.amazon.com/100-Startup-Reinvent-Living-Create/dp/0307951529

3. The 4-Hour Workweek by Timothy Ferriss

https://www.amazon.com/4-Hour-Workweek-Escape-Live-Anywhere/dp/0307465357

4. #AskGaryVee by Gary Vaynerchuk

www.amazon.com/AskGaryVee-Entrepreneurs-Leadership-Social-Self-Awareness/dp/0062273124

Glossary

App

Short for "Application". A computer program that can be downloaded onto a mobile device, including social networks, games, mobile tools, and much more.

Bio

Short for "Biography". A description in your profile that allows you the opportunity to give a little more information about yourself and your page. Up to 150 characters.

Caption

A description underneath each post that can be used to give context to the post, or simply show a bit of your personality.

Comment

An area beneath each post and caption in which any user, including the one who made the post, can add remarks about the posts. Comments can include hashtags and emoticons as well.

Direct Messages (DM's)

An inbox linked to your account where users can communicate with each other privately. Much like email or mobile texting, these messages are sent in real time to your inbox and allow users to privately converse with each other, whether they follow each other or not.

Engagement

The level of interaction between users and a particular post.

Filters

Various photo-editing presets that can be applied to a photo to alter its exposure, color balance, vignette, contrast, saturation, and more. These can be used both on the Instagram app and on 3rd party design apps.

Follow

You can "follow" another user's account, and any photos or videos that they post to their account will show up regularly on your home page.

Followers

Anyone who follows your account is one of your "followers".

Following

Anyone whose account you follow is somebody who you are "following".

Hashtags

Any word can become an active hashtag by placing a "#" symbol in front of it. Hashtags act as searchable content, and when attached to your posts allow other users to interact and connect with the relevant hashtags they are searching for. They are often associated with topics or specific trends, as well as used in marketing campaigns.

Home Page

A constantly updating feed of photos and videos posted by users that you follow. It is the first thing that shows up when you open the app.

Impressions

The total number of times your post has been seen (which includes multiple viewings).

Insights

Tools that provide information about your account, including metrics, analytics, and data about users who interact with your account.

Likes

A way to show interest in a post. You can double-tap it or click the "heart" symbol underneath the post to like it. Other users can like your posts as well.

Live Video

Video that is streamed in real time, which is connected to a user's page and viewable by their followers or the public.

Metrics

Data collected that measures a certain value on the app, contained in the "Insights" section.

Niche

A specific section or category of any given market, platform, or community.

Post

Any photo or video uploaded to Instagram, often including a caption and tags.

Profile

Your gallery of photos and videos. Users can view these by clicking on your account, follow you, or read your Name, Bio, and click on any links that you've provided.

Reach

The number of unique accounts that have seen a specific post.

Story

This feature lets users post photos or videos which will vanish within 24 hours, unless they are pinned as "highlights" on a user's profile page.

Tags

Placing the "@" symbol before any username will make that account clickable, so that other users will be brought to their account upon clicking. Additionally, locations can be "tagged" to a post.

3rd Party Apps

Any mobile applications that are not included on the Instagram platform.

Title

The "Name" of your profile, written above the Bio.

Unfollow

The act of clicking a link in order to remove a user from the list of those that you follow. Doing so will keep their posts from showing up on your homepage, and reduce your "following" list.

Username

The handle, or written name, which other users will use to identify you. It can include a few special characters, such as "_" underscores and "." periods.

Acknowledgments

My deepest gratitude to Annie Agnew, Scott Greenleaf, Axel Mansoor, Bobby Browning, the Curran family, Chris Adams, Bobby Galvan, and Atlee Feingold - you all lifted me when I was down and pushed me whenever I slowed (or was just being lazy).

To my wonderful family: my father, Rob, my mother, Karen, Mary Clare, Cory, Brian, Anthony, Esther, Mark, Karina, George, my grandmother, Shirley, and - last but certainly not least - my Grammy, Priscilla. Your constant love and support mean the world to me.

Lastly, a big thanks to the inspiring community of Poem Wars, to authors Tim Ferriss for *The 4-Hour Workweek* and Chris Gulliebeau for *The $100 Startup* - which served as priceless guides and motivators - and the saintly Julia Cameron for her book, *The Artist's Way*, which always kept me on the straight and narrow, no matter how large my doubts.

About the Author

R.J. Hendrickson was almost eleven when he was first found at the forest fringe of the Berkshires one particularly cold winter, accompanied by a lone female wolf who, in a solemn farewell, licked him on the cheek and was never seen again.

Under the care of human, non-wolf foster parents, his adolescent years were normal, even joyful - yet R.J. would often walk alone on snowy days, contemplating the forest and its mysteries in quiet knowledge that his true home was out there, among the frozen rivers and brambled thickets of his childhood, his pack forever lost to him.

Perhaps it was this, and a carnivorous appetite for the written word, that pushed him into his first foray as a poet. Soon his room was filled with the works of great literary men. For every Thoreau and Whitman who brought him back into contact with that natural world he knew so well, there was an Eliot and a Ginsberg to stretch and inspire his perception of societal living.

In his first public act of unrestrained artistry, he thrillingly recited his senior thesis poem to his high school assembly in a series of howls and phonetic vocalizations which would later be seen as a revolutionary reconciliation of wolf culture and the modern human condition. As with all true literary prodigies, R.J.'s creative vision was misunderstood, and the school immediately suspended him for disorderly conduct and "not following the prompt."

This early clash with the literary establishment would become the impetus for his life's work, a burning and unquenchable passion to bring acceptance and harmony to all who find themselves as outcasts of our society, spurned by the status quo and left to the wolves.

Made in the USA
Middletown, DE
13 September 2018